T0116942

Exploring Austria

Vienna and Beyond

Adrea Mach

iUniverse, Inc.
Bloomington

iUniverse books may be ordered through booksellers or by contacting:

iUniverse
1663 Liberty Drive
Bloomington, IN 47403
www.iuniverse.com
1-800-Authors (1-800-288-4677)

ISBN: 978-1-4502-7805-8 (sc)
ISBN: 978-1-4502-7806-5 (ebook)

Printed in the United States of America

iUniverse rev. date: 03/07/2011

Contents

****

1. INTRODUCING AUSTRIA: AN IMPERIAL LEGACY

This book is about adventures you are encouraged to experience directly, not just dry history. Still, in order to get the most out of them, a little background helps. Especially now, embarking on the 21ˢᵗ century, in which the country could be personified as a 'sleeping beauty,' just re-awakening from almost a century of shadowed slumber that began with World War I and the loss of her illustrious empire. Before that, in her prime, Austria dazzled the hearts of a vibrant "empire upon which the sun never set". Politically powerful and culturally alluring, Austria wielded influence over most of Europe. At the same time, her Viennese capital, home of the waltz, exuded a beguilingly feminine charm.

This short introduction will take us back in time to witness Austria's birth and trace how she arrived at where she is today, plus some bright promises for the future. There'll be cross references to each vignette included so that if you want to jump ahead, you can just skip to the adventure of your choice!

Austria: Odyssey of a Life Unfolding

From resources to Romans. If "appearance is everything," as some say, then Austria is especially fortunate, having inherited some of the best resources, in the form of splendid scenery that Europe has to offer: voluptuous snow-capped mountains to the west; verdant, fertile plains in the east. The lay of the land contributes to every country's history and just as the Alps provided protection against invaders (as well as strategic passes connecting north and south), so the welcoming Danube Valley opened its arms eastwards to embrace the rolling wooded hills and fertile plains of Bohemia, Moravia and Hungary that proved inviting to both invaders and settlers from the Stone Age onwards.

1

So inviting, in fact, that in the first century BC, the Romans "came, saw and conquered," founding the province of *Noricum* and establishing close links with contemporary Italy that flourish to this day. Roman Emperor Marcus Aurelius even put *Vindobona* (today's Vienna) on the map by succumbing to pneumonia in this remote Roman outpost in 180AD while his troops sought to beat back tribal invaders.

The Danube is another treasured resource. Europe's second longest waterway, emerging in Donaueschingen (today's Germany) and emptying into the Black Sea, almost 1,800 km away, and part of the continent's circulatory system, it has been a river that not only connects, but also protects.

Serving a similar purpose as the "Limes" (path), the fortified frontier of the Roman Empire in Europe, the Danube and the towns that grew up along it, like Vienna, marked the outermost north/eastern boundary of security, the last bastion between "civilization" and the "invading hordes."

For three centuries, the emerging Hapsburg empire was bounded by this virtual demarcation line, a 750-mile autonomous military frontier zone, mostly along the Danube, which depended less upon borders or fortifications than on the multi-ethnic "wild and warlike folk" that, for generations, successfully beat back waves of would-be invaders, and owed fealty only to the Emperor himself.

From christening to positioning. Austria's original name was "Ostarrichi", meaning "the Eastern Realm". A church document shows that Austria was thus "christened" only in the late 10th century as a child of the Babenberger family that ruled (after the Bavarians, Charlemagne and the Magyars), and brought several centuries (976-1246) of relative peace and prosperity—prerequisites for sound early development—to the area.

From the beginning, young Austria was not only well-proportioned but also well-positioned, sitting astride two strategic intersections. While alpine passes like the Brenner served as prime trading and military crossroads between north and south, the Danube linked up west with east.

To position herself optimally, Austria also opened another hidden treasure chest: her Salzkammergut. As early as 1,800 BC Bronze Age settlers discovered salt—the equivalent of today's diamonds—in the region around Hallstatt that gave its name to an entire age. Later the Romans, Slavs and Bavarians began to exploit this treasure, in 1460 creating the official "Crown Salt Lands" with their underground salt mines. The income created a substantial dowry for young Austria.

A precocious early bloomer, Austria began to emerge from obscurity when her 13th century "adolescent self" passed into the hands of one Rudolph von Hapsburg after the key Battle of Marchfeld (1276). Thus, this Swiss-born Hapsburg eloped with Austria, embarking upon a "marriage" that was to last for more than six centuries (1276–1918), bringing Austria into full flower at the height of her power. And it was much more than just "flower power".

For over 600 years, this "Austrian domain" acted as Europe's bulwark, not only between the Germanic and Latin worlds, but also against territorial and religious expansion, especially from the Muslim Turks to the east. Twice—in 1527 and then again in 1683—the Turks besieged Vienna. Had they succeeded, they would have changed the course of European history—indeed, even Western civilization.

To underscore how aware Europe was of its vulnerability, Prince Metternich coined the phrase, "Asia begins at the Landstrasse," which meant literally the "country road" that then stretched away from its city ramparts towards Hungary. Still, with crucial help from Hapsburg allies (e.g. 17th century Polish forces led by Jan Sobieski), Vienna withstood these sieges and Europe's eastern frontier was not breached.

On the contrary, an emboldened Austria went on the offensive, expanding in all directions to the very brink of achieving its aim of universal dominion, both secular and sacred.

"AIEOU"

"Austriae est imperare omni universo."
"It is for Austria to rule the entire world."
- Emperor Frederick III, 1452

Austria's Debut: "All the world's a stage": Beholding Austria's spectacular debut on the world stage, we can see in retrospect that it owed its emergence as a world power, not only to the House of Hapsburg, a rather dour, dutiful family with Swiss roots, but also to some very special qualities all leaders *must* embody—audacious vision, bold yet practical actions, and unshakable self-confidence. These enabled young Austria to expand its modest "Eastern Realm" into a far-flung imperial dynasty through centuries of wars, military and marital alliances, and purported divine sanctions.

Commitment to this vision, plus the religious fervor of the day, played a pivotal role. Thus, the 1452 crowning of Frederick III as Holy Roman Emperor by none less than the Pope himself legitimized the Hapsburg's claims to "preside by divine right as God's chosen dynasty over the entire civilized (Christian) world". The ambitious, far-sighted (and clearly megalomaniacal) Frederick III coined the Latin phrase that has been compressed into the vowel-list acronym "AEIOU", which translates into: *"It is for Austria to rule the entire world."*

Again, the rise and fall of nations is not unlike the rise and fall of rulers or, indeed, normal mortals. Austria in the 15th century was on her way up; similar to America on the eve of the 20th century. Today our sense of history-in-the-making turns prophetically towards the People's Republic of China, whose ascension on the world stage seems unstoppable, full of fervor and confidence. Perhaps even such contemporary superpowers could benefit from some lessons that Austrian history has to offer.

One of the lessons lies in the cultivation of a sophisticated sense of diplomacy. In the centuries following Austria's ascendance on the world stage, the Hapsburgs enhanced their repertoire of war, developing a unique diplomatic ability to preclude territorial battles by instead arranging politically astute marriages. Austria proved so good at this that it was crowned with the following epithet:

> *Bella gerant alii, tu, felix Austria, nube.*
> *Nam quae Mars aliis, dat tibi regna Venus*
>
> Let the strong fight wars. Thou, happy Austria, wed.
> What Mars bestows on others, Venus gives to thee instead.

The first such auspicious marital alliance took place in the late 15th century (1477) between Emperor Maximilian I and Maria of Burgundy. Austria's acquisition of the "cultural pearl of Europe"—Alsace, Lorraine and the Netherlands—laid the foundation for the Hapsburgs to become the continent's unrivalled dynasty. The next generation of Hapsburgs negotiated similar dynastic marriages. For example, Maximilian's son, "Philip the Handsome," married the Spanish Infanta, "Joanna the Mad," splitting the Hapsburg family tree into two strong branches, one Austrian, the other Spanish.

Thus, the Hapsburgs managed to achieve hegemony over much of Europe with minimum bloodshed and maximum matrimonial alliances. Behold, in the sequence of their acquisition, the list of sovereignties in the Hapsburgs' marriage records between 1415 and 1740: Portugal, Burgundy, Brittany, Bavaria, Castile, Aragon, Savoy, France, Denmark, Bohemia, Hungary, Mantua, Austria, Poland, Ferrara, the Netherlands, Tyrol, Palatinate-Neuburg, Lorraine, Brunswick, Saxony, Tuscany, Parma, Saxe-Teschen, Spain Naples, Cologne, Württemberg, Sicily, Nassau-Weilburg, Salerno, Sardinia, Belgium, Braganza, Liechtenstein, Saxe-Meiningen, Mecklenburg, England.

Pride Goeth before the Fall. Charles V, Maximilian and Joanna's son, ruled for almost 40 years (1519-56) over an empire that included much of today's Spain, Austria, Burgundy (France), the Netherlands, Germany, Italy, Eastern Europe, parts of the Caribbean and Mexico. Crowned in 1530 as Holy Roman Emperor by Pope Clement VII, Charles was figuratively "on top of the world." In addition to this secular "empire upon which the sun never set," the staunchly Catholic Charles also sought to "unite all Christendom under one scepter" from his El Escorial Palace in Spain. *Hubris.*

The immensity of Charles V's dominions was matched only by the immensity of his pretensions to world hegemony. Yet both were dashed by one single man—Martin Luther, who audaciously nailed his "Ninety-five Theses" to the wooden door of the Castle Church in Wittenberg (Germany) in 1517.

That single act unleashed the Protestant Reformation, whose concept of a personal god threatened the legitimacy of an Emperor "divinely sanctioned" and crowned by God's earthly interlocutor, the Pope. The Catholic Church rushed to retaliate. The brutal backlash of the Counter-Reformation found its low points in the draconian Inquisition and the decimating Thirty Years' War (1618-1648).

In the end, the Hapsburgs could not prevail against two consecutive threats: religious conflicts on the one hand, and territorial conflicts on the other. The latter culminated in a second devastating siege laid by the Turks in 1683 when all of Europe held its breath that Vienna would not fall. She didn't, but Austria was exhausted. This was the high point of her territorial trajectory.

Enlightened—and unenlightened—Despots. Despite a series of military setbacks, politically and socially, Hapsburg Austria was still maturing. The 18th century produced two both beloved and memorable Hapsburg rulers: Empress Maria Theresa, who as a female had to fight for her right to rule at all but then did so, and very ably, for 40 years (1740-1780), defending Austria against the rising power of Prussia. She was joined and then succeeded by her idealistic son Joseph II (1780-1790), who came to embody the image of the "enlightened despot" by placing the welfare of his subjects uppermost. Vienna was also "aglow" with enlightenment, intellectual and cultural vitality, emerging as an unmatched musical Mecca, with such composers as Gluck, Haydn and Mozart.

Ominously, the outbreak of the French Revolution in 1789 reverberated throughout the Hapsburg Empire. Austria lost much territory, not to mention prestige, when Maria Theresa's grandson, Franz II, was forced to abdicate his role as Holy Roman Emperor. A few years later, the situation was further exacerbated by the throes of the Napoleonic Wars during which much of Austria was occupied and the victor's 'spoils' bespotted its enemies in an intentionally degrading way by such acts as stabling French cavalry horses in magnificent Melk Abbey and obliging Hapsburg Archduchess Marie Louisa of Austria to be his second wife (after Josephine). She bore him a son, Napoleon II, King of Rome (1811-1832), who however died young of tuberculosis. .

Only after Napoleon's defeat and definitive exile could the Congress of Vienna (1814-1815), orchestrated by Austrian Foreign Minister Prince

Metternich, move to redraw the map of Europe. And at last there was a brief respite during this heady period when "the Congress danced" for two years to the waltzes of Strauss, father and son—while Austria produced an unprecedented crop of illegitimate children—and Vienna once again occupied the Western world's centre stage.

An Empire Past its Prime. Still, very fundamentally, the European balance of power had shifted. Austria struggled with the reality that the Hapsburg Empire had passed its prime and nothing would ever be the same again. The ideas of the Enlightenment, which had spurred the French Revolution, which, in turn, had spilled over into the Napoleonic Wars, had forever changed the *Weltanschauung* of Europe. Divine right was a thing of the past.

In 1848, a wave of proletariat revolutions swept Europe, with the people rising up against absolute rule of any kind ... although this was the *very* kind of rule upon which the Hapsburgs had built their empire. When 18-year-old Franz Josef ascended the throne in that same year and re-introduced absolutist rule, the stage was set for drama. Even though he ruled an incredibly long 68 years and, over time, became much loved by his subjects, Austria was sliding down the slippery slope.

Forgetting—except for Franz Josef and Sisi—her magic formula of weddings instead of wars, Austria became embroiled in a half-century of conflicts and fragmentation, losing in 1859 and again in 1866 against Prussia. Then, under pressure from the Hungarians and with energetic support from Empress Elizabeth, the once haughty Empire conceded to re-create itself as the Dual Austro-Hungarian Monarchy in 1867.

As the 20th century dawned, a series of secret alliances were being formed—Austria signing the Triple Alliance treaty with Germany and Italy while the future Allies—Britain, France and Russia—signed the Triple Entente. These two polarizing alliances laid the groundwork for the outbreak of the "Great War" that ensued in 1914. .

Living on Borrowed Time. *Fin de siècle* Austria lived in a surrealistic state of "nervous splendor," according to author Frederick Morton. The *coup de grace* for the 600-year-old empire was "the inevitable decline and fall of a dynastic supranational state unable to resist the tide of nationalism" sweeping Europe.

Thus, even against the audacious backdrop of avant-garde art by Klimt, Kokoschka and Shiele, and lulled by Mahler's mystical "Resurrection Symphony," back in the "real world," the Empire was fragmenting and falling apart. Like Humpty-Dumpty riding for a fall, once it did, even the Emperor could not put the pieces back together again.

Stoically, the aging Franz Joseph tried to keep the Empire alive through attention to detail and dogged perseverance (the good Emperor began his administrative day before dawn at 0400 in the morning). He did his best but still was left to bear three deaths that served as body blows to himself and his Empire: the suicide of his only son, Crown Prince Rudolf in 1889, the assassination of his beloved wife "Sisi" in Geneva in 1898, and the assassination of Franz Ferdinand, heir to the throne, in 1914 in Serbia.

Death ... and Rebirth. Austria herself ignited World War I—the "Great War" to end all wars—in August 1914 when Franz Josef signed the declaration against Serbia from his summer residence in Bad Ischl. But it was unlike any previous Austrian war. Four years of brutal trench-war bloodletting and an unprecedented number of deaths devastated all of Europe, especially the vanquished countries like Austria. Franz Josef died in 1916 and the debilitating losses, heavy reparations and, above all perhaps, a deep sense of shame and humiliation caused Karl I to abdicate in 1918, thus ending the Hapburgs' six-century old Empire. Austria's self-esteem and sense of identity had been struck what seemed a fatal blow.

Enduring 20 years as a truncated "orphan republic," a very vulnerable Austria was forcefully re-joined to Germany through the latter's *Anschluss* on 13 March 1938 when ***Austria*** as such ***ceased to exist***. Renamed "Ostmark", it was drawn into World War II (1939-1945) and, once again, after losing almost a quarter of a million soldiers, in addition to hundreds of thousands of civilians, Austria came out on the losing side.

Fortunately for her, the seeds of Austria's rebirth were sown in the darkest days of World War II. The Moscow Declaration of October 1943, to which the Allied Powers—the UK, US, France and the Soviet Union—were signatories, took the position that the Allies would "liberate Austria from its German yoke." Thus, they endorsed a principle that separated Austria's fate from that of Germany and offered it the option of re-acquiring its former pre-*Anschluss* 1938 borders at the end of the war. Austria was being granted a second chance—in fact, a second life. A rebirth.

And so it was, even if not immediately. Finally, after ten years of Allied occupation, the pivotal 1955 State Treaty—or *Staatsvertrag*—gave Austria back her independence. Even beyond Austria, the 15th of May 1955 remains a defining moment in post-war European history. In a rare display of quadripartite unity unmatched since 1945, the Four Powers joined with Austria to sign the agreement which restored its national birthright of sovereign independence lost 17 years before.

Then US Secretary of State George Shultz lauded this State Treaty *"a victory of reason and peace."* His contemporary counterpart, US Secretary of State Condoleezza Rice, said that the State Treaty was *"a settlement which provided the secure framework for a free and democratic Austria, neutral but deeply committed to Western liberal values, to thrive and prosper at the crossroads of Europe."*

For Austria itself, patriotically speaking, it was a first-rate experience; also for politicians of the "new Austria". As subsequent Chancellor Bruno Kreisky wrote in his memoirs, the return of the delegation from Moscow was *"the greatest day in my life"*.

All foreign troops were withdrawn by the following October—the date of 26 October henceforth serving as the country's National Holiday. The liberation of Austria was an accomplishment not to be underestimated, considering that none of the other Eastern Bloc satellite countries had been able to escape the Soviet Union's orbit. It was the 1943 declaration that saved Austria from further travails.

Austria Re-emerging. To the long-term observer, watching this odyssey is like witnessing the recuperation of someone who has had a near death experience ... *and survived.* The post-war years saw a slow but sure process of political consolidation, economic recovery and reconstruction and social development that brought stability and increasing prosperity to the country, its people and, most importantly, its spirit.

In commemorating the 50th anniversary of the end of World War II in 2005, the United States affirmed its pride in *"the role it played in helping preserve peace and stability in Europe for two generations after World War II."* America's post-war Marshall Plan (1947) *"played a central role in the development of a free and prosperous modern Austria,"* by making generous financial provisions. Austria received about a billion dollars over the years from the European Recovery Programme, investing it wisely in industrial and infrastructural projects, such as the Kaprun Dam.

Austria declared its "active neutrality" in 1955. As one of the United Nations' 51 founding members, it has also been successful in establishing the third UN centre worldwide in the Vienna International Centre, which houses the International Atomic Energy Agency, created in 1956 under the auspices of US President Eisenhower, to further the concept of "atoms for peace". The UN Industrial Development Organization, UN Office on Drugs and Crime and other UN entities also reside in the VIC. This has brought Vienna an influx of international staff, flair and political presence.

As a republic, today's Austria is thoroughly democratic—something the Hapsburg mentality could scarcely have entertained. The Government comprises a President, a popularly elected Chancellor and a two-tiered Parliament with proportional representation. Its carefully managed economy is based on a deeply rooted "social partnership" introduced in the 1970s by Chancellor Bruno Kreisky (1911-1990), one of Austria's and the world's most far-sighted statesmen. On the 25th anniversary of the State Treaty, he maintained that Austria had been able to re-create itself, albeit on the funeral pyres of multiple military defeats, and that this phoenix quality of being able to arise from the ashes demonstrated "a certain greatness, a sort of quiet *grandesse* ...which the Austrian has learnt from history and will hopefully remember for a long time."

"Actively neutral", the "new Austria" is also an active member of the Council of Europe, the European Union, the European Monetary Union and the Organization for Security and Co-operation in Europe. Although the days of Empire are over, the days of Union are just beginning. At last, with Austria's 1999 adoption of the Euro, Europe's single European currency, the future looks bright once again.

Remembering the Past: Even though the power is gone, some of the glory remains, immortalized in Vienna's architecture. Today the Imperial Hapsburg history is evident to even the most casual visitor to its 1.6-million strong capital city of Vienna. Just explore the historical treasure chest of the inner city with its intricate network of tiny medieval lanes and outdoor markets, with its palatial residences and spacious squares that embody the city's history. Or take a stroll around its resplendent Ringstrasse, which was built to replace the city's ramparts in the 1860s. Recall that the buildings that line this circular avenue—the impressive High Baroque Hofburg Palace and gardens, the twin Museums of Art and Natural History framing a statue of Empress Maria Theresa, the Greek-style Parliament, the neo-Gothic City Hall, the National Theatre and the University of Vienna—mark the circumference of the old city. Its expansion was part of the overall "face-lifting" that took place in the 1860s when Emperor Franz Joseph commissioned construction of the Ringstrasse where the city's ramparts once stood.

Looking toward the Future. While remembering her past lessons in diplomacy, Austria is now carefully cultivating her political neutrality in the international community and her pivotal economic position at the juncture of Western and Eastern Europe in the swiftly expanding European Union.

TODAY'S AUSTRIA AT A GLANCE

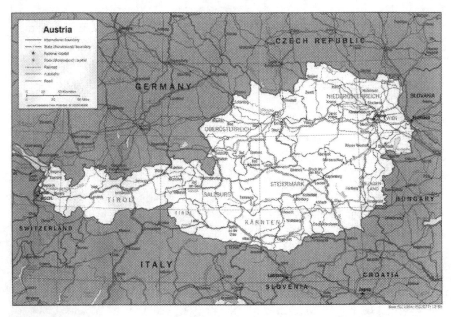

Geographically: Located in central Europe, today's Austria is a small landlocked country (Longitude 47 20 N, Latitude 13 20 E) of approximately 84,000 sq km (32,000 sq mi), not quite as large as the US state of Maine. Its 2,500 km of national boundaries surround it by eight countries: Germany, the Czech Republic, Slovakia, Hungary, Slovenia, Italy, Switzerland and Liechtenstein. In terms of elevation extremes, its lowest point is the Burgenland's Neusiedlersee (115m) and its highest is the summit of the Grossglockner (3,798m) between East Tyrol and Carinthia. Although tiny, Austria enjoys a key strategic location at the crossroads of central Europe with many easily traversable Alpine passes and valleys. The major waterway is the Danube that flows eastwards through Vienna.

Demographically: The population numbers about 8.2 million people, 67% of them between the ages of 15 and 60 and the majority living in the eastern lowlands. In terms of ethnic diversity and based on the most recent (2001) census, 91% are Austrian, 4% former Yugoslavs (e.g. Croatians, Slovenes, Serbs, Bosnians), 1.6% Turks, 0.9% Germans and 2.4% others. In terms of religion, 74% are Roman Catholic, 4.7% Protestant, 4.2% Muslim and 3.5% other. German is the official national language with other neighbouring languages, such as Slovene, Croatian and Hungarian recognized in the provinces of Carinthia and Burgenland. Both literacy (98%) and life expectancy at birth (79) are high, with males living an average 76 years and females, 82 years based on 2006 estimates.

Politically: Once the formidable European center of power for the Austro-Hungarian Empire, Austria was reduced to a small republic after its defeat in World War I. Following its "union" with Nazi Germany in 1938 and subsequent post-World War II Allied occupation after 1945, Austria's status was in limbo for a decade. The 1955 State Treaty ended the occupation, recognized Austria's independence, forbade unification with Germany and declared the country's "perpetual neutrality" as a condition for Soviet military withdrawal. The 1991 collapse of the Soviet Union, Austria's entry into the European Union in 1995 and into the EU Economic Monetary Union in 1999 have paved the way for it to become a prosperous, democratic country.

Governmentally: The federal Republic of Austria is a constitutional democracy created in 1955. The National Day—October 26th— commemorates the passage of the law on Austria's "permanent neutrality". Legally, the civil law system is based on Roman law. Legislative acts are judicially reviewed by the Constitutional Court and there are separate administrative and civil/penal supreme courts. The country is divided into nine administrative districts or "Bundesländer": Burgenland, Kaernten (Carinthia), Niederösterreich (Lower Austria), Oberösterreich (Upper Austria), Salzburg, Steiermark (Styria), Tirol, Vorarlberg and Wien (Vienna).

Economically: With its well-developed market economy and high standard of living, Austria is closely linked to other EU economies. It also benefits from strong, renewed commercial relations with the banking and insurance sectors of central, eastern and southeastern Europe. Boasting a large service sector, sound industrial sector and small but highly developed agricultural sector, Austria's EU membership has drawn foreign investors attracted by its access to the single European market and proximity to new EU economies. Due to higher growth across Europe, Austria grew 3.3% in 2006. To meet increased competition, Austria will continue restructuring, emphasizing knowledge-based economic sectors and encouraging greater labour flexibility and participation by its aging population. In keeping with Austria's commitment to permanent neutrality, military expenditures amounted to only 0.9% of GDP, allowing the country to invest more in areas like public health care, education, housing and social services.

TODAY'S VIENNA AT A GLANCE

"Vienna is special."

'Wien ist anders' – Vienna is special. Since this slogan for the Austrian capital was coined many years ago, it has become a popular catchphrase in Vienna – and rightly so. As Mayor and Governor of this city Mayor Michael Häupl is in the fortunate position of not having to compromise between quality of life and economic growth. Vienna has produced a perfect combination of a high life style, a thriving economy, and ecological sustainability – as shown year after year in international city rankings.

Vienna prides itself on being "special"—that is, slightly quirky with a wry sense of humour. But Vienna is also progressive in a laid-back, socialist sort of way that looks out for its citizens "from the cradle to the grave". That's what makes the daily quality of life for virtually all classes so pleasant. In preparation for Austria's turn at the EU Presidency in 2006, new statistics were gathered for the city that send the following messages loud and clear:

- **Vienna is "green":** More than 48% of the City of Vienna is "green", either in the form of the Vienna Woods or agricultural land, often used for the cultivation of vineyards that overlook the city from the west. In comparison, Zurich has only half that (24%) and Munich only 36%.

- **Vienna is seasonal:** Although in the temperature zone, Vienna registers fairly extreme temperature variations: the highest was 37.6° C in 2003 while the lowest was -18.1° C in 1996.

- **Vienna is sunny (sometimes):** In Spring 2005 Vienna registered 217 daily hours of sunshine; but in August received the doubled amount of average rain.

- **Vienna is demographically balanced:** In 2005, Vienna's population numbered 1.65 million, 55% of which were women and 18.7% of which were non-Austrians. The division according to age groups is becoming more balanced over time (pie chart graph showing the following: as of 2031, it is predicted that 15.5% will be 0-15 yrs; 18.4% will be 15-30 yrs; 21.8% will be 30-45 yrs; 19.0% will be 45-60 yrs; 16.1% will be 60-76 yrs; and 9.1% will be over 75 years old).

- **Vienna is growing:** For the first time since World War II, the number of live births exceeded the number of deaths (i.e. by 750 for a total of 16,750 in 2005). Immigration increased by about 20% to 78,000 in 2004 although the percentage of approved citizenship applications decreased by 25% (16,354 in 2004 to 12,240 in 2005).

- **Vienna is socially supportive:** The City of Vienna helps career-mothers through support for Day-Mothers and child care groups. Over half (53.5%) of children between 1.5 – 3 years obtain places in a crêche. Long-term financial social support altogether accounted for some €144,000 in 2004. There are 27 shelters for the homeless and 164 bed for female victims of domestic violence.

- **Vienna is health-conscious:** There are 12,300 doctors, 310 pharmacies and 41 hospitals or clinics with a total of 13,505 beds. Its drinking water is delicious and nearly 100% from mountain springs.

- **Vienna values education:** There are 1,630 kindergärten for ca. 36,000 children; 428 basic schools for 103,473 students; and some 114,000 students enrolled in universities throughout Austria.

- **Vienna supports culture and sports:** All told, the City of Vienna has 170 cinemas (many with original language films), 150 museums, 70 live theatres, 67 libraries, 20 daily or weekly newspapers and 157 sports centres. And, by the way, Vienna danced its way through 582 different balls in the course of the 2004/5 winter season!

- **Vienna is business-friendly:** Approximately €350 million was available in 2006 for work-supportive programmes. Over 910,000 of the total 1.6 million population were employed in Vienna in 2005 with an unemployment rate of less than 9%.

- **Vienna contributes economically to Austria's success:** Less than 20% of the Austrian population (in Vienna) contributes more than 25% of the country's economic output. Austria's GDP stood at $36,980 per capita in 2005, ranking it 12th globally out of 184 countries evaluated by the World Bank. *(Source: http://www.finfacts. ie/biz10/globalworldincomepercapita.htm)*

- **Vienna is visitor-friendly:** In 2005 alone, Austria registered almost nine million overnights—more than equal to its own population! Over seven million were from outside Austria and, of these, the majority were from Germany (2.0m), Italy (0.653m) and the USA (0.60m).

- **Vienna is conference-friendly:** In 2005 Vienna hosted 366 international conferences—more than one for every day of the year—with over 160,000 participants and almost 800,000 overnights in this city of lights.

- **Vienna pushes public transportation:** Almost 750 million people used Vienna's state-of-the-art public transport system in 2005. Thus, the ratio of private cars decreased to only 481/1,000 population.

- **Vienna remains "red".** Once decried for its "red" or strongly socialist political leanings, it is now increasingly acknowledged that this is the Vienna municipal government's way of looking after *all* of the city's citizens, not just the rich ones who (anyway) need little looking after. Thus, the SPÖ (Socialist Partei Österrreich) obtained 55: 100 mandates and 49% of the popular vote in 2005.

- **Vienna is regaining its economic clout:** In comparison to other EU capitals, as of 2002 Vienna ranked sixth for net gross regional product after London, Luxemburg, Brussels, Stockholm and Paris … and before at least 17 other European capitals in terms of the cost of living.

- **Vienna has one of the highest qualities of life ANYWHERE!** The "Quality of Life Survey 2005" conducted by Mercer Consulting Group awarded Vienna first place for quality of life amongst all European cities and third place worldwide; in 2009 it came in first worldwide.

Vienna: *The perfect place to live, enjoy and explore life in Austria and Europe!*

MAIN AUSTRIAN HOLIDAYS, SEASONAL EVENTS, FESTIVALS

DATE	PUBLIC HOLIDAY	EVENTS	FESTIVALS/PLACE/ EXPLANATION
1 January	New Year's Day	New Year's Day	Kaiser Ball (New Year's Eve): Vienna Hofburg
6 January	Epiphany	Perchtenläufe	Perchten. Bad Gastein
End January		Opera Ball	Vienna Opera House, followed by a six-week long ball season through Fasching
February*			Fasching/Mardi Gras/ Carneval - Nationwide
Mar/Apr*	Good Friday		Friday before Easter Sunday
Mar/Apr*	Easter Sunday		Christ's Resurrection
Mar/Apr*	Easter Monday		Monday after Easter Sunday
1 May	Labour Day		
May*	Ascension Day		40th day after Easter Sunday
May*	Whit Sunday - *	Narcissus Festival in Bad Aussee	Pentecost (Pfingsten) 50 days after Easter
May*	Corpus Christi	Hallstatt Lake Procession	2nd Thursday after Whitsun
May-June		Music Festival	Annual Vienna events
June-July		Danube Festivals	Krems, Wachau. Dance, music, arts and Summer Solstice celebrations
July-August		Salzburg	Salzburger Festspiele
July-August		Mörbisch	Operetta Festival on the Neusiedler See
July-August		Bregenz	Lakeside musical extravaganza

15 Aug	Maria Himmelfahrt		Maria's Ascension
Sept-Oct	Wine harvest	Wachau, Burgenld	Processions, fireworks, wine-tastings
26 October	Austrian National Day		Since 1955 when Austria declared neutrality & regained its independence after WWII
1 November	All Saints' Day		
Nov-Dec	Advent	Christmas markets	Four Sundays preceeding Christmas; Nationwide
8 December	Immaculate Conception		
25 December	Christmas		
26 December	St. Stephen's Day		

*Moveable religious holidays. Sources: Wikipedia, Michelin Green Guide Austria

2. EXPLORING VIENNA AND ITS ENVIRONS

According to the travel industry, the latest trend is "slow travel"—that is, not the 10-day/10-city "been there, done that" frenzy—but its opposite, the leisurely "getting to know you" note. That's what this section is about—eco-friendly savouring of the city on foot, by horse-drawn carriage, tram, bike, boat or "Tschu-Tschu", all with Vienna's famed "Gemütlichkeit".

In this and the following chapter, a number of the shorter references have been drawn from Wikipedia.

Excursions within the City

TIP: GET YOUR "WIEN KARTE"!

For savings and convenience's sake, visitors can purchase a three-day "Vienna Card" for **€ 16.90** that entitles you to **72 hours of unlimited free travel** on ALL Vienna public transport (i.e. undergrounds, trams and city buses). Showing this ticket also gets you discounted entry to some 150 city museums, as well as discounted purchases in designated department stores, restaurants, cafés and wine bars. See details on the booklet accompanying the "Wien Karte", which can be purchased at hotels, tourist information centres, ticket sales and information offices belonging to the Vienna transport authorities.

Thematic Vienna Walking Tours

Vienna may be a world capital but, with its population of only 1.65 million, it is a relatively small and compact city whose historical centre and numerous pedestrian streets are easily negotiated on foot. For this reason, Vienna's certified City Guides (check for their red-and-white badge!) offer over 50 walking tours in German and English—from "Vienna at First Glance" to "A Life of Love and Lust: Johann Strauß and his Women" to "Spirits, Ghosts and Vampires: Creepy Vienna". Something for every taste and all to be found in the monthly flyer "Wiener Spazier-gänge/Walks in Vienna" distributed at all Tourist Information Offices or under www.wienguide.at. Below just a few samples:

1. **Vienna at First Glance:** This overview tour of the main sights in Vienna's Inner City leaves on foot at 1400 from the first district Tourist Info at the corner of the Albertinaplatz and the Maysedergasse for a 1.5-2 hour walking tour. English/German: Friday, Saturday, Sunday and French on Saturdays at 1000, leaving from the same location.

2. **Vienna Altstadt:** Two walking tours leaving from St Stephen's, one towards the Hofburg, the other towards the Old University; both highlighting key sites of Old Vienna. History and anecdotes from the Roman outpost of Vindobona through the Turkish sieges and hidden treasures of 600+-year old Hapsburg Empire that ruled much of Europe from Vienna.

3. **Vienna's Coffeehouses:** Vienna owes its "thanks" to the Turks for bringing coffee beans, together with their 1683 siege, to the city. The Austrians created a coffee cult of their own, each major coffee house from Hawelka to Landtmann to Demel's linked to certain get-together traditions from literary to military and far more. Delve into this fascinating Viennese world!

4. **Musical Vienna:** Visit the (many successive!) homes of Mozart, Beethoven and Schubert, learn of their successes, foibles and failures, their living habits, love lives and last hours. Learn about other musical venues, such as the world famous State Opera, the Musikverein and the Konzerthaus.

5. **The Imperial Apartments:** Of the 2,600 rooms in the Hofburg, several dozen belonged to Emperor Franz Josef and Empress Elisabeth (Sisi) and are duly imprinted with these two iconic

personalities: Franz Josef's is amazingly Spartan for one of his rank while Sisi's features gymnastic equipment and one of the first "imperial bathtubs". You can also see the Imperial staircase and magnificent Imperial porcelain and silver collection.

7. Private English-speaking Guides

Becoming a certified Austria Guide requires two years of intensive training and several more to build up a reputation and clientele. Below are some English-speaking multilingual guides that the City of Vienna and the AWA can recommend if you want to organize a private tour:

Helga Chmel
Tel (+43) 01 505 92 69
Helga.chmel@stadtfuehrungen.at

Jeffrey Hebe
Tel. (+43) 01 87 67 111
hebegolf@netscape.net

Alexander Ehrlich
(+43) 0676 520 24 94
guide@ahre.at, ahre.
austriaguide@gmx.at

DDr Anna Ehrlich
(+43) 0676 922 77 73
office@wienfuehrung.at,

Maria Husa
Tel. (+43) o185 97 13
Husapr.geographie@univie.ac.at

Eleonore Neubacher
Tel. (+43) 01 369 64 01
vienna-tours-leonor@aon.at

Brigitte Timmerman & Family
Tel. (+3) 01 774 89 01
info@viennawalks.com

Felicitas Wressnig
Tel. (+3) 01 504 52 39
guide-felicitas@chello.at

Christine Colella
Tel. 0699 88 45 32 63
Christine.colella@chello.at

Peter Jirak
(VIC Hiking Club guide)
Tel. 01 333 67 28/02287 4423
peterjirak@gmx.at

The Prater: You don't even need a guide for this—and the kids will love it! Once a royal hunting preserve in medieval times, today the Prater is home to Vienna's outdoor amusement park—the so-called "Wurstelprater" with all sorts of stalls, beer gardens, carousels and futuristic rides. Take a nostalgic ride on the historic 19th century Ferris Wheel (Riesenrad) that is part of the city's skyline, as well as the film, *"The Third Man"* that made it famous. The Prater is also an enormous 60 sq km park, its chestnut-tree lined Hauptallee being the place to venture forth with horse and carriage to see and be seen during the Imperial Hapsburg's heyday. Horses are still a charming addition, with horse-racing at the Freudenau and trab-racing at the Krieau ... and not to forget the huge Ernst Happel Soccer Stadium and exhibition grounds where travelling shows like André Heller's *"Africa! Africa!"* are set up in huge circus tents.

Trams Tours: To spare your feet and get a sense of the historic ramparts of the Old Vienna, nothing beats hopping aboard the bright yellow **Ring tram** (with commentary) and making a full round of the Ring. Your path traces precisely that of the city's old ramparts, which were demolished in the 1860s by Emperor Franz Josef to create this lovely broad circular avenue surrounded by the gems of Imperial Vienna's architecture. During the tourist season (April - October), you can also take an **"Oldtimer Tram"** that leaves from the Karlsplatz at 1130 and 1300 on Saturdays, Sundays and public holidays for a one-hour tour.

Eco-friendly Fun

Fiaker Tours: Looking for something memorable and romantic ... or just a ton of fun for the kids? Then take an hour-long horse-drawn carriage ride through the inner city by day or by night. Drivers usually provide a fascinating running commentary. You'll find fiaker stands at St. Stephen's, on the Heldenplatz in front of the Hofburg and on the Albertinaplatz behind the State Opera. Ask the fee first as these can be quite pricey: €95 an hour on average.

Cycling Tours: Vienna has over 1,000 km of marked cycling paths for you to enjoy (see the brochure *Tips for Cyclers* from Vienna Info for maps and details). Bikes can be rented at numerous locations in the inner city, on the Danube Island (Donauinsel) and at the Prater. *Pedal Power* 3-hour cycle tours are also offered from May - September (Tel. 01 729 72 34).

In fact, one of the nicest rides is to pick up a free "City Bike" from the 1ˢᵗ district's Schwedenplatz, pedal downstream (not *in* the water though!) along the Danube Canal, then cross the pedestrian bridge into the lovely, leafy Prater and stop for a coffee or G'sprizten at the Lusthaus (Pleasure House) before cycling back—this is especially magical when the fuschia and white chestnut trees bloom in May. Another is to take the U-1 to the Donauinsel stop, where there is a bike and roller-blading rental shop, and criss-cross to your heart's content up and down the shores of the Danube and Old Danube.

Inner City Segway Tours: Something new, this 3-hour commentary tour by segway takes you effortlessly around the Ring and through the inner city and helps orient you to Vienna, its history and its scenic beauty. Reservations at www.CitySegwayTours.com or Tel. 01 729 72 34 required for all tours. Minimum age: 12 years old.

Boat Tours: Embark from the Schwedenplatz on a circular 2.5 hour cruise (with refreshments) from the Danube Canal (where the main Danube once flowed before being diverted), through the locks and onto the Danube-proper, where you get a spectacular view of both sides of the river overlooked by the Kahlenberg and Leopoldsberg, before negotiating the upper locks at Nußdorf back to your point of embarkation. Tours April – October operated by the DDSG Blue Danube Boat Trips (Tel. 01 588 88 00). The *Vindobona* is a boat designed by the late Viennese artist and architect Friedensreich Hundertwasser.

… and speaking of Hundertwasser and eco-friendly living!

Austrian visionary painter, sculptor, architect and spiritual ecologist Friedensreich Hundertwasser (Friedrich Stowasser) was born on 15 December 1928 in Vienna. Perhaps Austria's best-known—though always controversial—independent artist, he travelled, lived and worked in diverse locations throughout Europe, the East, North Africa, Australia and New Zealand. Consistently working with spiral motifs, primitive forms, spectral colors and repetitive patterns, some of his most powerful works are to be found in Vienna and farther afield in Austria. He believed art to be a religious experience, always opting for spiritualism over rationalism. His intention was to offer his viewers "a glimpse of Paradise, created while the artist is in a dream state". His self-bestowed name means "Hundred Waters-Kingdom of Peace." He died in New Zealand in February 2000 and was buried at sea.

Lonely Planet introduces Austrian "Enfant terrible" artist and architect, Friedensreich Hundertwasser, this way: *"Ever dreamed of burying your house in dirt, planting some trees on the roof and getting back to nature? If so, a visit to stately Vienna will show you the different ways that one man has turned that dream into reality. Austrian architect Friedensreich Hundertwasser dedicated his life to destroying fascism through architecture."*

Another Austrian-bred Jewish genius, though regarded by many as a "burned-out hippy", Hundertwasser lost 69 of his relatives in WWII's Nazi concentration camps. Subsequently he attempted to do away with what he called "the tyranny of the straight line", claiming that modern cities were ugly "because the ruler and T-square limit possibilities". He insisted that "man is shielded from nature by three levels of insulation: cities, houses and clothes" and tried to limit the latter impediment, not least by running round his buildings naked on occasion.

Hundertwasser's goal was to make cities—not to mention people—more harmonious and environmentally friendly. Thus, his art emphasizes the curvaceous, irregular and uneven. Especially on Vienna's bourgeois boulevards, his buildings are daring and provocative, the best-known work being the "outrageously" colourful, organic ***Hundertwasser House,*** Vienna's most original public housing project built in 1977 that attracts more than a million visitors each year. No wonder. A wild jumble of building blocks, in brightly coloured blues, ambers, whites and pinks, with foliage poking through at the most unlikely places, people from far and wide come to see it; what they can't see are the private apartments' interiors filled with grass, flowers and hanging gardens.

Address: Löwengasse 41-43, (Kegelgasse), Vienna 1030
Neighbourhood: 3rd district - Landstrasse
Phone: +43 0900 90 0913 (Within Austria)
Nearest Station: Tram O, N
Web: http://www.hundertwasserhaus.at

Another place of equal, if not even more, interest is the KunstHausWien, a former factory rebuilt as a permanent exhibition centre for Hundertwasser's works, as well as rotating exhibitions of contemporary art. Irregular multi-coloured elements of glass, metal, bricks, wood and ceramic tiles lend a unique look to this complex opened in 1991 just a few blocks from the Hundertwasser House itself. By the way, the ground floor and garden also feature a delightfully "green" restaurant and book/souvenir shop. Another boon to the city's skyline is to be found in the beautified district heating system at Spittelau, which is prominent on the Danube Canal.

Address: KunstHausWien (1000-1700 Daily)
Untere Weissgerberstrasse 13, 1030 ViennaTram N, O: Radetzkyplatz
Phone: Tel. 01 712 04 91
Web: www.kunsthauswien.com

Source: http://www.wiegels.net/ tuerme/neu/02107.jpg

Air Tours: For a bird's eye view, hop aboard a small Cessna 210 single-engine plane for an exciting 30-minute airborne circuit above the city with the foothills of the Alps on the horizon. Contact Vienna Aircraft Handling at Schwechat, Tel. 01 700 722 204. But be warned that these are not cheap!

Bus Tours: Business as Usual

If you are interested in participating in pre-organized bus tours, below is a list of the primary bus tour operators in Vienna and its environs. Be aware though that while the tours may be less expensive and personalized than privately organized ones, they may also be conducted in several languages simultaneously and thus have less time for fuller explanations in English.

Bus & LimousineTour companies

CityRama Tours
1010, Börsegasse 1
Tel. 01 534 13-0
Email: office@cityrama.at
www.cityrama.at
Daily: 0630 – 2000 (hotel pick-up)

Elite Tours
1010, Operngasse 4
Tel. 01 513 22 25
Email: travel@elitetours.at
www.elitetours.at
Mon-Sat 0900-1600 &
through ticket agencies

European Touring Programme – Carey Limousine
1300 Vienna Airport, Arrival Hall
Tel. 01 7007 333 40
Email: office@viennasightseeing.at
www.ecarey.com
Deluxe private city tours. All credt cards accepted.

Vienna Sightseeing Tours
1040 Stelzhammergasse 4
Tel. 01 712 46 83
www. Viennasightseeingtours. com
Check website for office hours.

Tyrolian Tours
6372 Oberndorf; Tirol
Tel. 05356 631 34
Email_ info@tyroliantours.com
www.tyroliantours.com
Specially tailored winter/skiing holidays in Tyrol (Kitzbühel area) for English speakers. 200 lifts in a 20 km radius. Accommodations range from self-

VIC Ski Club
Vienna International Centre
Tel. (01) 26026 Ext. 5547.
Email: info@vicskiclub.org
www.vicskiclub.org
Organizes weekend to full week ski trips in English for members (€10pp or €15/ family).
Buses usually leave the VIC at 1700 on catering apartments to 5-star hotels with all meals. Fridays and return Sunday around 2130.

Six "On -- and Off -- the Beaten Track":

1. **Hop On/Hop Off: Vienna Sightseeing Tours.** For those whose time is limited, you can join one of the Vienna Sightseeing buses that leave every half hour from the Staatsoper and see the major sights (the Ringstraße with its "ornaments", the State Opera House, the Hofburg and its Heldenplatz, the Museums of Art and Natural History, the Parliament, the City Hall, the Burgtheater, Vienna University, the Votiv Church, the Stock Exchange, St Ruprecht's, the Danube Canal, the Prater, the Stadtpark, the Schwarzenbergplatz and the Hotel Imperial) with explanations in both German and English—all in one hour. You can use this "hop on, hop off" ticket however you like.

2. **The Vienna International Centre (VIC):** Opened in 1979 on the banks of the Danube, the VIC was at that time Vienna's largest construction project, meant to house over 4,000 staff at the UN's third centre worldwide after New York and Geneva. Multilingual tours of this international complex take place daily at 1100 and 1400 and by reservation. Tel 01 26060/3328.

3. **Freud's World:** Sigmund Freud, the "father of psychoanalysis", was born, studied and practiced here in Vienna, developing his pioneering theories of the Ego, the Superego and the Id, plus many other theories on the repressed sexuality beneath Vienna's proper Victorian façade. The Freud Museum in his former residence helps to bring the fantasies of *fin-de-siècle* Vienna alive. See also the well-researched but tongue-in-cheek book, *Sigmund Freud: The Whole Truth (The Couch Speaks!)*. Freud Museum in the Berggasse 19, 1090, Vienna. Times: Daily 0900 – 1700. Prices for entrance and guided tour: €3,50–8,00. Tel. (+43) 01 319 15 96 or office@freud-museum.at

4. **On the Trail of *"The Third Man":*** This famous Orson Welles spy film, based on the book by Graham Greene, was filmed in Vienna in the 1950s and has become something of a classic cult film. The 30-minute tour takes you on a spooky underground round of Vienna's sewer system and is full of espionage-like surprises. Participants must be at least 12 years old and all should wear sturdy, closed-in footwear. Bookings at MA30- Wien Kanal, Tel. 01 585 64 55.

5. **The Palaces: Schönbrunn**, today a UNESCO World Heritage Site, was once the summer residence of the Hapsburgs. Located in what used to be wooded countryside that is now well within Vienna's boundaries, it is automatically included in some city bus tours. In case you want more time, take the U-4 directly to Schönbrunn and enter by the impressive main gate to purchase your ticket at the right side box office. Then you can take a 2+-hour tour that includes: the Imperial apartments where Marie Antoinette spent her childhood and the seven-year-old Mozart played before some of Europe's crowned heads; the Schloßpark with the "beautiful fountain" for which Schönbrunn was named, the Gloriette on a hill above the park and the Coach House. During Advent, one of the loveliest and most authentic Christmas Markets is also staged here in the front courtyard.

   Schloß Belvedere, although closer to the city center, was another summer residence, its two palaces linked by a formal garden built for the renowned Hapsburg field marshal and art collector, Prinz Eugen—that is, François-Eugène, Prince of Savoy-Carignan (1663-1736). An outstanding example of Austrian Baroque architecture, it is here that the milestone State Treaty was signed in May 1955, giving Austria back its freedom in exchange for eternal neutrality. Today the Belvedere houses the world's richest collection of paintings by Austrian art nouveau painter Gustav Klimt, including his world famous canvas, "The Kiss".

6. **Schlumberger.** By now, you might be really tired and in need of a pick-up treat! Then how about a tour of the Schlumberger Sekt enterprise whose caves stretch far underground in Vienna's northwestern suburb of Heiligenstadt—no wonder they call it "holy/holey city"! For a guided tour, contact: Schlumberger Wine and Sekt Cellars, Heiligenstädterstr. 43, Tel. +43 1 368 60 38-0, Website: www.schlumberger.at

Vienna's Periphery: "Wienerwald" and "Heuriger-Hopping"

Vienna owes not a little of its charm to its surrounding greenery/scenery and to its manageable size (i.e. only about 1.65 million residents in 2007 compared with 10 million for greater London and 12 million for greater metropolitan Paris). The city is both saturated with, and surrounded by green, its "green lungs" on the west being the leafy Vienna Woods (Wienerwald), splashed with a swath of the Danube's blue (at least when the sun shines at the right angle).

You don't have to go far at all to get a taste of scenic rural Austria: from the Danube Valley (with its more than 500 castles and fortified monasteries), to the vibrant Vienna Woods and its 7 sq km of vineyards that extend right into the city—by the way, making Vienna the world's largest wine-growing city!—you can easily treat yourself to a pastoral respite. Below are a series of inviting excursions around Vienna's periphery.

The Vienna Woods: Few European capitals have the luxury of such an enormous green belt (1,250 sq km) of protected woodland wilderness right at their doorsteps, which has inspired scores of musicians from Schubert to Schönberg. Put on the musical map by Strauß's lilting waltz, "Tales of the Vienna Woods", this arc of mostly deciduous trees stretches in a graceful crescent from north to southeast along the entire western periphery of the city. And, yes, thanks to prescient zoning laws, the woods still look much as they did in Strauß's day—gently rolling, invitingly green, criss-crossed with marked hiking paths and dotted with "Gasthöfe" and "Heuriger" serving the year's new wine.

VIENNA'S HEURIGER: UNIQUE IN THE WORLD!

"Heuriger"? The only truly authentic ones in the whole world are said to encircle Vienna. What are they anyway?

Well, to start with, they're two things (not that you're seeing double already!). Technically, they're the liquid product ("Most", "Sturm" or "Neuwein") of the most recent winegrape harvest while, socially, they're the "Buschenschank", the traditionally rustical place where this "comfort for body and soul" is dispensed. An institution unique to Vienna, according to those in the know, the Heuriger amicably reflects that world-renowned collective "Gemütlichkeit" of which the Viennese are justly proud. "Just accept it, don't analyze" says one convert, "it'll do you good."

The real Heuriger, according to German Gastronome Wolfram Siebeck's book, *Die Heurigen von Wien*, serve as "an extended living room" where people know and greet each other, where they saunter in after work or on a leisurely afternoon to "relax and forget their everyday cares." The idea is *not* to get drunk; it's just to get *mellow*. The Heuriger's ambience acts as a psychological "Ventil", an outlet of the sort that even the Viennese father of psychoanalysis, Sigmund Freud, might have frequented and, ideally, prescribed.

Vienna, with its green belt of vineyards and woods, is surrounded on three sides by some 500 such Heuriger. On the northwest and west are the best-known Heuriger of Grinzing, Sievering, Döbling, Nussforf and Neustift; in the southwest and south are Mauer, Perchtoldsdorf and Gumpoldskirchen and, in the north are the so-called "advanced-level Heuriger" of Jedlersdorf, Strebersdorf and Stammerdorf that offer the highest quality wine in the most authentic, non-touristic settings.

In Vienna, Grüner Veltiner grapes grow right on the hillsides within the city limits so people don't have far to go to sample each year's harvest. The Heuriger tradition—which claims to be unique in the world—began in the 18th century. Empress Maria Theresia, the first female Hapsburg ruler, justifiably known for looking after the well-being of her subjects, followed by "enlightened despot" Joseph II, issued edits allowing the local Viennese vintners to serve their tart "new wine"—almost invariably white—from grapes harvested in the current wine year (up until St Martin's Day in November of the following year). As a signal, the vintners hung a pine branch above the entrance to indicate that they were open, thus the expression, "Ausg'steckt."

It soon became apparent that wine alone, without any accompanying food, brought about rampant intoxication, brawls and bad hangovers. To assuage the situation, the edicts were expanded to include self-service buffets with bread, cold cuts and cheese spreads. Thus these simple Heuriger, set amidst Vienna's vineyards, were soon flourishing from April to October. Today, of course, many commercial Heuriger are open year round and outdo themselves with full-course warm meals but the tradition is simple fare in a rural outdoor setting, usually amidst the vineyards or under the shade of chestnut trees. Here families (including children, grannies and dogs!) are most welcome and playgrounds are often provided (only the children aren't served wine but Obi or Almdudler, fruit-and-herb-based based non-alcoholic drinks). Whole afternoons can be spent this way, sometimes serenaded by "Schrammelmusik", songs sung in unmistakable Viennese dialect by crooning gentlemen playing violins and zithers, accordions and guitars. The Viennese love their music and their leisure ... and their wine. You have to experience them yourself first hand. So let's do just that!

Northwestern Vienna Woods: Some of the most authentic, and highly recommended, feature plain open air picnic tables plus dreamy views over the Danube and are nestled into the 19th district hillside vineyards around the Kahlenberg. You can heuriger-hop on foot between April and October between several of them, driving or taking the U4 to Heiligenstadt and then the Bus #38 to Kahlenberg or (if you prefer an uphill hike to whet your appetite) the S-Bahn from the Franz-Josefs Bahnhof to Kahlenbergerdorf and stroll, down or up as your choice may be, through the vineyards.

Vienna Heuriger Express: We do something delightfully different! Descending from the D Tram's last stop in Nussdorf, we cross the street to hop aboard the picturesque open air "Heuriger Express" that departs April-October every hour on the hour between 1200 and 1900 for an hour-long jaunt through Vienna's woods and vineyards with stops at the Kahlenberg, the famous wine village of Grinzing and others along the way. For more details, please see the website http://www.heurigenexpress.at/html.

To the tune of taped Viennese "Lieder", we ascend through rolling vineyards to the top of the Kahlenberg for a panorama view over Vienna, then hop off on the way back down at **Sirbu** (Tel. 01 320 5928), a single Heuriger nestled under trees in the midst of the vineyards from which our wine comes. We hear only Viennese, not a single "foreign accent" (our own excepted!) and enjoy our wine, Kümmelbraten (roast pork belly with caraway seeds) and Topfenstrudel. Crossing between two vineyards, we walk down towards the Danube until we reach the hidden-away **Hirt** with its twin rustic terraces, one facing the woods, the other the river. These two Heuriger complement each other timewise as Hirt is open as of noon daily, including weekends and holidays, whereas Sirbu opens only at 1500 (the traditional mid-afternoon Heuriger opening time) and is closed on Sundays and holidays. Both are authentic and very atmospheric. Several hours later, we rejoin our Heuriger Express, which drops us off at **Reinprecht's** in Grinzing for one last "Viertel" as the lanterns in the garden wink on and we are treated to a live violin and accordion serenade of "*Wien, Wien, nur Du Allein…*"

Another well-kept secret up here is **Zawodsky** (Reinischgasse 3) which can be reached with tram 38. Unpretentiously authentic, its boasts a panoramic view over the city and an artistically unkempt garden of apple trees. Moving down into the residential 19th district, **Hengl-Haselbrunner** (Iglaseeg. 10) in Döbling is considered one of the best Heuriger in terms quality and charm while Heiligenstadt's **Mayer am Pfarrplatz** (Pfarrplatz 2) is closely associated with Beethoven's life and work.

Getting there: Literally dozens of Heuriger stand side by side in the hilly villages of Grinzing, Neustift, Sievering and Kahlenberg and most can be reached by public transportation (Trams 38, 39, Buses # 37A, 38A, 39 and 40A respectively. It's good not to have to worry about driving home

Southwesten Vienna Woods: Heuriger abound in the southwesten Vienna Woods as well although you more often need a car to get there. Some of our favorites are in …

Perchtoldsdorf, or "P-dorf" for short, was first settled many centuries ago and vineyards dotted these hills since the 11th century. Long a fortified medieval township when the Turks overran the Vienna countryside in the 16th and 17th centuries, it was the scene of a bloody slaughter of local inhabitants. The tower was built on the north side of the marketplace and next to St. Augustine's parish church between 1450 and 1520. Today Perchtoldsdorf is one of the classier suburbs of Vienna where you can go on long hikes through woods and vineyards, ending the day in one of the typically inviting local Heuriger, a few of which are listed below.

• Rabl	Elisabethstr. 27	Tel. 01 86 983 77	Irregular; check times
• Barbach (86 pts)	Rudolfgasse 8	Tel. 01 869 83 78	weinbau-barbach.at
• Kas Nigl (84 pts)	Elisabethstr. 10	Tel. 01 869 83 76	Irregular; check times
• Mohrenberger	End of Fehnerweg	Tel. 01 869 83 75	Ausg'steckt May – Sept
• Neumayer	Sonnbergstr. 89	Tel. 01 869 86 81	Open every month

North of Vienna: "Heuriger for Connoisseurs". No more Vienna Woods. No more Biedermeier cinema scene Kitsch. We've crossed the Danube north of Vienna to get to the "Geheimtip" (insider tip) Heurige of Jedlersdorf, Strebersdorf and Stammersdorf. This is the real thing and gets top points when rating all of Vienna's Heuriger in terms of the quality of the wine and buffet, the garden and overall ambience. On Siebeck's scale of 100, the following Heuriger earn top points:

• Fuchs (93 pts)	Jedlersdorferplatz 20	Tel. 01 292 20 20	Every other month from Feb.
• Breyer (88 pts)	Amtsstr. 15, J'dorf	Tel. 01 292 41 48	Irregular; check times
• Eckeret (88 pts)	Strebersdorferstr. 158	Tel. 01 292 25 96	Open every other month

EXCURSIONS NORTH OF VIENNA

Stift Klosterneuberg Tel (02243) 411 212
www.stift-klosterneuburg.at

Now a pricey suburb tucked between the Vienna Woods and the Danube, the town of Klosterneuburg was the Vienna of its day under the Babenbergers who moved their court there from Melk early in the 12th century. The imposing Augustinian Abbey, destined to be Karl VI's El Escorial of Austria before the money ran out, nevertheless thrives to this day and has many property holdings in Vienna and Lower Austria. Tours of the square, church, cloisters and imperial apartments are offered in German and English (1000 – 1700 daily) and, on St Leopold's day (15 November), there is something really special that is great fun for young and old: "Fasselrutschen"! This means climbing by wooden stairway to the top of one of the Abbey's enormous old wine casks and sliding down the other side.

Burg Kreuzenstein
Tel (0664) 173 3445 or Tel. (0664) 422 5363 (H. Lenhart)
www.kreuzenstein.com .

Open daily April – October 1000 – 1600.

Located in Leobendorf just north of Vienna, Burg Kreuzenstein perches on a rocky promontory overlooking the Danube. Perhaps a perfect place for a private Halloween party, this is an authentic re-creation of a castle destroyed by the Swedes in the Thirty Years' War (1618-1648) and a fun Sunday family excursion, especially for those who find medieval history fascinating. The castle itself sports a true-to-life moat and drawbridge, a collection of armor and medievally furnished rooms. Guided tours are offered from 1000 and 1600 in German between April and October. For special arrangements, such as tours in English or off-season openings, call (02262) 661 02 to make advance arrangements.

Getting there: Drive north on the A-22 Autobahn to Korneuburg, then follow the signs to Leobendorf or take the Schnellbahn S3 from the Landstrasse (Wien Mitte) to Leobendorf station. It's a 30-45 min. (uphill!) hike through woods and vineyards to reach the castle.

EXCURSIONS SOUTH OF VIENNA

Laxenburg is an idyllically charming little village and site of one of the three former Imperial Summer residences, originally called the "Blue Court". It boasts a castle surrounded by a large lake and extensive park with walking and bridle paths where, for example, Empress Elisabeth ("Sisi") spent her honeymoon with Franz Joseph in 1854 and Crown Prince Rudolf was born in August 1858. Before that, in 1713, the Alte Schloß (Old Castle) is where Emperor Charles VI signed the "Pragmatic Sanction" that permitted Maria Theresa to ascend to the throne where she reigned successfully for 40 years (1740-1780).

Since 1972 the village of Laxenburg has been home to the International Institute for Applied Systems Analysis (IIASA) whose premises border on the castle part, a lovely place for a leisurely walk and boat ride with playgrounds along the way (alas, no bikes allowed). Leave yourself half a day and include a visit to the castle and its outdoor restaurant on the water!

Getting there: Laxenburg is located 16 kilometers south of the center of Vienna, along the south-bound A2 Autobahn. Exit at the Wr. Neudorf exit, take a left at the first light. Signs will then guide you to Laxenburg. If you prefer not to drive on the highway, you can go directly south from the center, on the Laxenburger Strasse (Route 16), which brings you through the countryside and several small towns to Laxenburg. For public transportation, take U1 or Tram 18 to the South Train Station (Südbahnhof). From there, take Bus #566 to Laxenburg. (€1.50 each way) that departs from the Südtirolerplatz 25 and 55 minutes after each hour. The trip takes 30 minutes. Buses do not always say "Laxenburg," but mostly "Eisenstadt" so ask the driver whether the bus you are boarding is going to Laxenburg. Get off in Laxenburg at the stop called "Franz-Josefs-Platz".

Liechtenstein Castle
2344 Maria Enzersdorf
Tel. 02236 47 2222 or 0664 301 6066
Email: infor@burgliechtenstein.at
www.burgliechtenstein.at
Daily: April – October 0930 – 1700

Entry €4 for adults and €2,30 for children (6-16). Group and senior discounts available.

About 15 km south of Vienna, this castle was built in the early 10th century by the Liechtenstein family and was part of Disney's "Three Musketeers" backdrop in the 1990s film. You can tour on your own or arrange in advance for a paid guided tour in English. There are several artificial ruins on the grounds and well as a playground with lots of open areas and walking paths. The Burg restaurant and buffet are also open on weekends.

Getting there: Drive south on the A-2 autobahn direction Graz and turn off towards St. Pölten/Linz (A-21). Then take the Gießhübl exit and turn left, following signs to "Burg Liechtenstein".

Lake Grotto (Seegrotte)
2371 Hinterbrühl
Tel. (02236) 263 64
Email: office@seegrotte.at
www.seegrotte.at

Open daily April – October 0900-1200 and 1300-1700; November – March 0900-1200 and 1300-1500; Sat., Sun., and holidays until 1530 (call for English tour times). Entry fee: €5 for adults, €3 for children.

Created as a gypsum mine back in the mid-1800s and eventually closed due to flooding, despite being pumped dray to build jet fighter fuselages before it was destroyed at the end of World War II. Today the tour of Europe's largest underground lake is offered as a year-round guided tour but bring warm clothes as the temperature hovers around only 9° Celsius, even in summer.

Getting there: This excursion is combinable with the Liechtenstein Castle, which is close by, or you can take a train to Mödling, then the bus 364 or 365 direction Hinterbrühl and get off at the grotto.

Gumpoldskirchen (Lower Austria); A2 Southautobahn

Located at the foot of the Anninger—a lovely walk up will *work* up an appetite—this village with the hard-to-pronounce name is another picturesque "heuriger heaven" on the so-called "Wine-hiking-road" (Weinwanderweg) that winds its way from the crest of a panorama view hill above Mödling through the vineyards south of Vienna. The most famous wine-growing village south of Vienna, it is deservedly well-known for its white wines and summer wine festival when all traffic is banned and the town becomes one big outdoor restaurant with musicians playing and people waltzing in the streets. In the fall and winter, try the Benediktinerkeller with its cozy underground heuriger with candlelit brick vaulted ceilings and a wooden slide that the kids can slide down.

Baden
www.baden-bei-wien.at English language website)

Baden is located at southern end of Helenental, about 26km from Vienna on the south autobahn. The town traces its origins as a thermal spa town back to Roman times when its mineral hot springs were first used to treat rheumatism, arthritis and circulatory conditions. It later became one of the Empire's most fashionable spas, reaching its apogee during the 19th century Biedermeier period when Emperor Franz Josef frequented it each summer. Musicians like Beethoven, Strauß and

Lanner also composed in Baden and it later became a summer operetta capital.

Although occupied by Russian forces for ten years after World War II (1945-55), it has now regained some of its former lustre. The Kurpark and Strandbad are worth a family visit, especially during the hot summer months, as there are also many cycling paths in and around Baden and the Helenen Valley.

Getting there: You can drive on the A2 Southautobahn, take the Badenerbahn train or the Baden bus from the State Opera in the first district (see transportation chapter).

Hikes with the VIC Hiking and Mountaineering Club: One of the Vienna International Centre's many registered clubs, the aims of the Hiking Club are "to encourage and to provide opportunities for hiking, mountaineering and other similar outdoor activities; and thereby to infuse the spirit of adventure and create love and interest in nature's beauty, its fauna and flora among the staff members of international organizations, their families and friends." Although full membership (€20/yr) is open only to persons employed with international organizations or diplomatic missions in Vienna and to retirees (€15/yr) from Vienna-based international organizations, guests can join individual hikes for €3-10/outing. **Hike Leaders** are volunteers from different countries with different hiking styles and ways of organizing trips. Do not hesitate to contact hike leaders (outside of office hours if possible) if you want more particulars about a hike before deciding to participate. The season's **Hike Circular** can be downloaded from the Internet http://www.geocities.com/vichiking, by emailing to request it from n.wonisch@iaea.org or calling Nancy Wonisch (Tel: 2600-21134 / 01 714 38 05) to have a circular mailed. Below are a few hike samples to whet your appetite!

Summer Evening Walk: Cobenzl to Hermannskogel to Sievering
"Some enchanted evening …" After work, take off for another world right at your doorstep. Just drive—or take the U4 to Heiligenstadt and Bus 38A—from there towards Kahlenberg. Get off at the Cobenzl Caférestaurant, a neo-Baroque land-mark (right). Ascend the Stadtwanderweg 2 (city hiking trail) by the Jägerwiese (Hunter's Meadow) to the Hapsburger lookout tower

on top of the Hermannskogel (542m), Vienna's highest "peak". Take in the panorama over the city of Vienna as the lights blink on before descending to the quaint village of Sievering, founded by Bavarian settlers in the 9th century and today a popular and picturesque vine village. Refresh yourself at the Heuriger Koller (Sieveringerstr. 269A, Tel. 01 440 22 24)

Day Hike: Mauerbach to Hagenbachklamm

Undertaken in the spring just when the orchards are blooming, the bees and butterflies fluttering about, the song birds serenading and the Waldschenke awaiting us with a delicious lunch in the garden before a march through the magical Hagenbachklamm, this is a real outing for all the five senses!.

About 15 of us have assembled ourselves in Hütteldorf at the end station of the U4 at 0800 on an April Sunday morning with Peter, our thoroughly charming Austrian guide from the Vienna International Centre's Hiking Club. We take bus 249 for a 25-min ride that deposits us in idyllic Mauerbach. In his liltingly accented English, Peter briefs us and off we go on our trek that takes us from the Carthusian monastery in Mauerbach for two hours or so through the springtime fresh landscape to the top of the Tulbingerkogel on the northern edge of the Vienna Woods, where we climb the Leopold Figl Outlook Tower for a panoramic view.

Then we descend through the woods until we reach the **Waldschenke** Staar (A-3001 Mauerbach, Tel. 02273 73 88 http://www.waldschenke-wienerwald.at), today a gentrified heuriger nestled in wooded splendour that dates back to the 17th century and has now become a welcome escape for Sunday wanderers and "Prominenz-in-hiding". After a leisurely lunch, we visit an adjacent Easter handicrafts exhibit before setting out for an afternoon exploration of the scenic "natural jewel" of the Hagenbachklamm (gorge) that winds down through the woods, at last arriving in St. Andrä-Wörden where we take the train back to Vienna.

"Wanderbares Wien"—Wandering around Vienna

This delightful brochure produced by the City of Vienna presents over a dozen easy hiking trails, together with maps and access information, right on the city's doorstep. Among others, hikes on the Kahlenberg, Leopoldsberg, Jubiläumwarte, Sofienalp and through the Prater, as well as circular trails all around the city, are featured. If you are one of those A-type achievers, you can even get a "Wanderpass" stamped for each completed hike, which will earn you a pin ("Wandernadel") to wear as a feather in your hiking cap! Tel. 01 277 550 or 01 4000 97947).

EXCURSIONS EAST OF VIENNA

Carnuntum is the Latin name for the ruins that mark the original Roman outpost (the military garrison Vindobona is the site of present-day Vienna) on the Amber Road that extended south from the Baltic Sea. Today's remains include two amphitheatres and the Heidentor, a massive gate that stands all alone on a grassy meadow. You can also visit the museum in Bad Deutsch-Altenberg that houses ancient Roman artefacts found on the site. For info, contact 2404 Petronell-Carnuntum and Bad Deutsch-Altenburg, Tel. (02163) 33 77, Email: info@carnuntum.co.at, www.carnuntum.co.at

The Neusiedlersee, a unique ecological phenomenon of a lake, lies farther afield in the province of Burgenland and the border to Hungary. Reachable by a 45-minute train ride from Vienna's South Train Station to Neusiedl am See, it is great for sailing, windsurfing, cycling, wine-tasting and enjoyng the annual summer operetta festival that takes place on a stage over the lake at Mörbisch. For more details, call Burgenland Tourist Information (Tel. 02682) 633 840 or www.burgenland.info or see *Exploring Austria: Vienna and Beyond.*

EXCURSIONS WEST OF VIENNA

The Vienna Woods Looking at a map (Michelin, p. 382), all you will see on the western periphery of Vienna is green. And so it is. Either woods or vineyards or both.

Vienna Panoramas: For striking views of the city, take to the hills overlooking it. A drive along the Höhenstraße, a partly cobblestone road that winds through the Vienna Woods, is the best way to do it. Several panorama restaurants (e.g. Fischerhütte, Cobenzl) line the road, in addition to the promontory lookout points of the **Kahlenberg** (where a large new hotel complex has just been built) and the **Leopoldsberg**, both of which overlook the Danube. Take the 38A bus from the terminal of the U4 Heiligenstadt that will deposit you on the top of the Kahlenberg, from which you can walk to the Leopoldsberg and back or take a steep ridge trail that brings you down to Klosterneuburg.

Mayerling, through the site of a scenic hunting lodge, it is also the site of a tragedy—the double suicide of Crown Prince Rudolf and his 17-year-old mistress Maria Vetsera in January 1889—after a falling-out with Emperor Franz Josef. To this day, mystery continues to surround this demise of the heir to the Imperial throne. Today a Carmelite convent occupies part of the site in addition to rooms commemorating Crown Prince Rudolf, which can be visited.

Heiligenkreuz
Guided tours 1000-1700 daily
Tel (02258) 8703
www.stift-heiligenkreuz.at

The "Holy Cross" Cistercian Abbey, begun in the 12th century to house an alleged relic of the cross, is one of the most impressive around Vienna, combining Romanesque, Gothic and Baroque architecture. On special occasions, you can witness Gregorian chant being sung by the monks who otherwise work in the fields and orchards. An interesting, if tragic, sidelight, Crown Prince Rudolf's mistress Mary Vetsera, who committed suicide with him in 1889, is buried in the village cemetery.

When in Vienna ...

Unlike the fanatically athletic Tyroleans, the Viennese like a little leisure with their exertions (or vice versa). So it has become something of a tradition for the typical Viennese family—mom, dad, the kids and the dog—to take to the woods on Sunday for their weekly "wandern" or hiking. So that everyone knows exactly what they're up to, the rule is to dress the part: that means intrepid high-alpine hiking boots, corduroy knickers with knee-socks (usually bright red), a red-and-white checked shirt, leather vest and, not all too infrequently, a cocky Tiroler hat with a mountain-goat swatch plus the all-pervasive raingear and "Studentenfutter" (nuts and raisins) tucked away in a sturdy rucksack.

After letting the dog off its leash and setting out at a brisk pace, they might even break into a few bars of some old Wanderlieder (hiking songs), usually to a brisk march tempo. But it won't be long before Papa's tummy starts to growl or Mama and the kids, not to mention the panting Labrador retriever, get thirsty. So, after maximum one hour, they stop for a morning snack of coffee and buttered Kaisersemmeln (white rolls); then, after rambling for at most another hour, it's time for a proper lunch so they either pack out their picnic at a long "trestle table" under the trees or stop in at one of the dozens of Gasthöfe along the hiking paths. There they recover from their exertions with a typical Sunday lunch of Fritattensuppe (clear soup with thin pancakes cut lengthwise into strips), the ubiquitous Wiener Schnitzel from pork or veal (which, by the way, owes its origins, not to Vienna but to Milan), pommes frites (which, as the French name suggests, are also not truly Austrian in origin), and mixed salad of potatoes (yet again!), cucumbers, kraut and tomatoes ("Paradiser" in the local dialect). This hearty meal may be washed down with beer but, unlike their German cousins, the Viennese are more likely to choose wine—a "G'spritzter" of tart local white wine laced with soda. Then course, "Apfelstrudel und Melange (coffee with milk)" for dessert, considering the strenuous afternoon ahead.

So off they go, at a somewhat slower "digestif" pace, strolling along beneath a canopy of sun-dappled birch and ash trees, perhaps ascending to the Anninger (428 m), the Vienna Woods' highest "summit" where a lookout/ transmission tower invites to a ladder "diretissima". After that, it's all downhill—to the next Gasthof, in this case, the Richardshof that sits picturesquely at the edge of the woods overlooking a broad meadow and the vineyards of Gumpoldskirchen. Time to replenish! The dog gets a bone and a bowl of water, the kids order Sacher or Malakovtorte and the parents have another go at something sweet as a reward for their robust day in nature. No wonder that, after such a day of "wandern" (from one gasthof to the next), the scales show an extra half-kilo despite all that exercise!

Schallaburg Renaissance Castle

Lower Austria: 10 minutes from Melk just off the Westautobahn
Entrance: €7. Guided tours €2.50 daily in German from 1000-1700
Advance arrangements for English-language tours required. Tel. 02754 6317.

No other region in Austria boasts as many turreted fortresses and castles from centuries past. The Schallaburg, located just a stone's throw from magnificent Melk Abbey, ranks among the finest Renaissance castles north of the Alps. The core of the fortress dates back to the Middle Ages, but today's characteristic appearance dates from 1572, when the prosperous Lose Steiner dynasty built a manor for themselves modeled on the Italian palazzo of the time. Striking terracotta mosaics depict vivid scenes from mythology while the castle's historic Mannerist gardens feature historic roses, ornamental trees and bushes, herbs, and typical Renaissance apple orchards. There is an adventure playground in the form of a huge smoke-spewing dragon outside the castle gates that invites children to slide from his mouth, climb up and down inside its body, and hides many secrets.

The Schallaburg is also well-known for its annually changing, cultural-historical and archaeological exhibitions, from the Mongolians and Egyptians to the Crusaders (2007) and the North American Indians (2008). Finally, the restaurant comprises two spacious halls and a rustic weapons cellar with plenty of room for events of all kinds, including wedding, anniversaries and company parties.

ÖBB Kombi-Ticket: A Packed Adventure

Leave your car and map at home and try this train-bus-boat-train combination offered by the Austrian Railway. You buy your €42.0 ÖBB Kombi Ticket (including all entrance fees) up front. The times are somewhat flexible but, to get the most out of a very full day, start early! Here's the way we did it:

Train from the South Train Station (Südbahnhof):	Dep Vienna 0740	Arr Melk 0904
Shuttle from Melk to Schallaburg Castle	Dep Melk 0915	Arr castle 0930
Tour of the Schallaburg & gardens		
Shuttle bus back to Melk	Dep castle 1100	Arr Melk 1130
Tour of Melk Abbey and lunch		
Danube boat trip through the Wachau	Dep Melk 1350	Arr Krems 1530
Explore Krems (incl museum visit)		
Return by train to Vienna	Dep Krems 1803	Arr Vienna 2004 (Franz Josefs Bahnhof)

This Kombi ticketoffer runs throughout the high season. Confirm times and prices with the ÖBB by calling Tel. 051717 and ask for regional train information.

3. FARTHER AFIELD: EXPLORING AUSTRIA

Encircling Vienna: Lower Austria

Vienna is encircled by the province of Lower Austria (*Niederösterreich*), one of the country's nine federal states or *Bundesländer*. With a land area of 19,174 km² and a population of 1.6 million people, Lower Austria is the largest, and in terms of population second only to Vienna (which also is a federal state in its own right).

Geographically, Lower Austria is called thus because it is located farthest downstream on the Danube River, which flows through it from northwest to southeast. Surrounding Vienna, it shares borders with Slovakia, the Czech Republic, and the other Austrian states of Upper Austria, Styria and Burgenland.

Not to be compared with the dramatic scenery of the snow-capped High Alps, Lower Austria is more "comfortable", its hilly areas alternating with broad plains, its alpine foothills alternating with the idyllic Danube landscape.

Vienna Woods: This region is the Viennese's favourite place to relax and also provides a preferred residential area on the city's periphery. The landscape is varied: the Danube graces the gates of the the elegant Austrian capital; deciduous forests cover the hills, and in the south is the so-called "Thermenregion" (Thermal Region) with famous spa towns like Baden and Bad Vöslau, and wine villages like Gumpoldskirchen.

Wachau-Niebelungengau: The Wachau is one of the oldest cultural landscapes in Austria and is said to be one of the most beautiful riverside landscapes in Europe. In December 2000, the whole region was declared a UNESCO World Cultural Heritage site. From Krems to Melk, the

Danube Valley covers a length of 36 km. Over the course of countless centuries, the steep, terraced vineyards and the small romantic villages with many historical sights attract visitors from around the world.

Lower Austria Pre-alpine: "The Wonder World of Magic Mountains" is the area's epithet for the southern and most alpine part of Lower Austria. The region starts a few kilometres south of Vienna and extends all the way to the Styrian border. In the southwest, the last alpine peaks form a natural border for the region: the Hochwechsel (1,574m), the Semmering (1,523 m), the Raxalpe (2,007 m), and the Schneeberg (2,076m), Lower Austria's highest mountain.

Mostviertel: This region is also called "Austria's Orchard" because of its abundance of fruit trees (e.g. apricots, apples, cherries), especially in the soft-hilly landscape along the Danube. Hikers, cyclers, mountainbikers and kayakers feel right at home here. The varied landscapes, the proud four-cornered farms nestled in lush natural surroundings, the countless cultural sites and leisure opportunities all contribute to making the Mostviertel a memorable experience.

The Waldviertel (Forest Region): Hills, broad fields and rich meadows, mysterious forests, moors and over 1,000 pristine rivers and ponds characterize the Waldviertel landscape, in addition to over 300 ruins and intact castles, palaces and abbeys. The Ice Age left behind countless "Restlinge" (leftovers) or "Findlinge" (erratic blocks)—boulders and rock formations that are millions of years old. They are the stuff of many a magical story.

The Weinviertel (Wine Region): Picturesque "Kellerstraßen" or "cellar streets" typify this region, also described as being full of "villages without chimneys". They fit perfectly into the partly flat, partly hilly landscape of Austria's biggest vinticultural region with over 18,000 hectares of vineyards. Romantic vineyards, orchards and vegetable fields in the Marchfeld, wide patches of nodding sunflowers or yellow rapeseed extend between the villages.

The Danube Valley: With a length of 2,826 km, the Danube is Europe's second-longest river after the Volga; for about one-eighth of its overall length (360 km), the Danube is Austrian. Starting at Passau on the German border, it sweeps in majestic curves through Upper and Lower Austria and the well-known Wachau wine-growing region, down past the Austrian capital, Vienna, to enter Slovakia just above Bratislava. Four national capitals are located on the Danube, attesting to its economic importance.

For residents of Vienna and its environs, Lower Austria invites you to explore its many treasures. The tourist office of the state of Lower Austria has dozens of publications, some of them in English. One we can recommend is *"Land der Wanderer: Die Schönsten Wanderungen im Weiten Land"* with 38 different detailed hiking routes. Another recommendation is to get yourself a €45 *Niederösterreich Card*, which provides free entry into almost 200 excursion destinations. Contact: Tel. 01 536 10-6200, Website: www.niederoesterreich.at, Email: info@noe.co.at.

Austria's Scenery at your Fingertips

Landscape, Climate and Water Flow

Austria is an alpine country with 62% comprising mountainous terrain; the remainder is hilly, with low-lying plains to the East. Alpine geological formations run in a predominantly west-east direction, with water draining north to the Danube and south to the Drava/Drau. The gradient of the Austrian Danube is circa 0.4 ‰, much steeper than in Lower Bavaria and the Hungarian Plain. Austria's continental climate displays high precipitation rates in Alpine areas (up to 3,500mm/yr). Austria contributes 46.3 km³/yr (< 25%) to the direct flow of the Danube.

> **Did You Know …?** Austria signed the Danube River Protection Convention as long ago as 1994. Its capital, Vienna, is the location for the ICPDR (International Commission for the Protection of the Danube) Secretariat.

The Danube: Austria's Main River

The Danube is by far the major economic, geographical and cultural fluvial force in Austria. Draining over 96% of the country's territory, the basin is home to 7.7 million people. In a country dominated by mountains, the flat lands provided by the rivers are of great significance for agriculture, human settlements and infrastructure. Still, Austrian territory accounts for only 10% of the total area of the Danube Basin.

Natural highlights include **the Wachau Valley**, a UNESCO World Heritage Site and outstanding example of a fluvial cultural landscape bordered by mountains; the Donau-Auen National Park, a protected floodplain area with a still relatively intact ecosystem linking Vienna and Bratislava; the Thayatal National Park, an impressive protected area on the River Thaya (Austrian-Czech border); and the Neusiedler See, also a UNESCO World Heritage Site consisting of a large, shallow lake, more than half of which is dominated by reeds.

Austria's Mountains

At the heart of the High Alps, Austria actually has more mountains percentage-wise (66%) than any other European country, including Switzerland (although the highest Swiss peaks are about 1,000m higher than the highest Austrian ones). Topographically, Austria is divided into three areas: in the middle are the High Austrian Alps with their snow-capped summits (i.e. the Großglockner at 3,798m is Austria's highest) and National Park, which lie mostly in Tyrol, East Tyrol and Voralberg; the northern Limestone Alps (e.g. Kaisergebirge, Dachstein), which lie mostly in Tyrol, Salzburg and Upper Austria and overflow into Bavaria; and the southern Limestone Alps (e.g. Carnic Alps and Karawanken), which today lie on Austria's borders with Italy and Slovenia. The foothills of the High Alps (e.g. Styria, Carenthia and Lower Austria), lie largely in Lower Austria and reach all the way to Vienna's doorstep. So let's highlight a few of them here.

Foothills of the Alps: Vienna's "Hausberge"

Semmering: Imagine that up until 1854, the only way to get over the Semmering Pass (1291m)—the highly frequented route between Vienna and the Adriatic ports of Venice or Trieste, which were then still part of the Austrian Empire—was on foot or by horse-drawn carts! Humiliating for the all-powerful Hapsburgs! And inconvenient for the voyagers! Something had to done—and it was. Something of pioneering significance!

Under the (later knighted) Venetian engineer, Carlo di Ghega, some 20,000 foreign laborers were set to work for six years (1848-1854) to complete Europe's first standard gauge mountain railway, connecting the already existing rail links at Gloggnitz in the northeast and Mürzzuschlag in the south.

A stunning feat of construction for those days, the track passed through 15 tunnels, over 16 Romanesque-style viaducts and more than 100 smaller bridges on a gradient of 1 in 4 to 5 for 60% of its 41km total length.

In 1854 the Semmering Railway was inaugurated by the newlyweds Emperor Franz Josef and Empress Elisabeth, a high point, literally and figuratively, in the Hapsburg's 600+-year reign.

Nostalgia Train ("Erlebniszug"): Although the line was electrified and modernized in 1956, you can re-trace this journey even today, leaving Vienna's South Train Station for a 1.5 hour trip (0814-0957) that features a quaint old train on the original railway route that brings you within a few hundred metres of the Semmering Pass, with its wonderful ski slopes (and a World Cup race) in winter and golf courses and hiking trails in summer. The Semmering is known for its exceptionally sunny climate. Price: €36.40 regular or €20.20 with a "Vorteilskarte" (Advantage card for the train). You can also consult Tel. (02639) 2212/247 for more information on Austria's Nostalgia trains and boats.

Traintrack Hiking Trail: The hiking trail follows the original path the workers used in building the railway and you can hike along it for anything from 1.5km (Wolfsbergkogel) to 21 km (Payerbach) or 23km (Gloggnitz). Along the way, be sure not to miss the panorama view from the top of the outlook tower at Doppelreiterkogel. For more details and a brochure with map, contact the Semmering Tourist Office, Tel. 02664 20025, Email: semmeringtourismus@aon.at, Website: www. semmering.at

Raxalpe: If you took the route from the Semmering to Payerbach (above), then you will have found yourself not far from the foot of the Rax cable car in Reichenau an der Rax. This cable car was Austria's very first when it was built in 1926! It will take you with minimum exertion up to the high plateau at 1,547m from which you can undertake any number of "hut-hopping" hikes between 10km and 16km in length, stopping along the way at the Ottohaus, Karl Ludwig Haus and Hapsburg Haus, scattered about the high plateau.

Be aware though that, even though the Rax is one of Vienna's favourite "Hausberge", it is a *real* mountain with challenging rock-climbing routes and sometimes severe weather conditions. Be sure to come equipped with the proper hiking boots, raingear, water and snacks in case the hike turns out to be more strenuous than you imagined! For more details, see www.raxseilbahn.at

Schneeberg: "Snow Mountain" translated into English, Lower Austria's highest summit (2,076m) is just that, at least in winter when its snow-clad silhouette can be seen all the way from Vienna on a clear day.

You can climb it! Winter or summer! Either on foot all the way from the bottom or (in summer only) with the help of the "Salamander" rack railway that takes you within "summit storming" distance of the top. If you're a purist, start at Losenheim and hike up to the Sparbacher hut (there's also a chair lift, but we won't tell!). Then take the Fadensteig up a steep ridge that brings a vertigo-free you up over the ridge and to the summit in 3-5 hours, depending on your climbing condition ... and the weather.

In winter, extremists also shoulder-load their skis (my Tyrolese husband did!) and, once at the top, free-skied down the Breite Ries or Lahning Ries. But for "Normalsterbliche" (normal mortals), hiking through the wind-swept snow up to the Fischerhütte for a respite over a hot "Huttensuppe" and then hiking down in thigh-deep snow to the Kienthaler hut and back to Losenheim was quite enough! For more details, see www.schneebergbahn.at.

Biking paths along the banks of the "Beautiful Blue Danube": This 350km cycling path between Passau and Vienna on the Austrian section of the Danube ranks as "Europe' best-known and most-loved cycling route." Picturesque farms, glorious abbeys, tranquil untouched valleys, fertile plains and steep vineyards weave a diverse scenery. The Danube loop at Schlögen, Melk Abbey and the romantic wine-producing

Wachau region are all irresistible! Get yourself a *Cycline* Danube Bike Trail Cycling Guide. Tel. 43 2983 289820. Email: cycline@esterbauer.com. Their website is: www.esterbauer.com.

Advent hike through the Johannesbachklamm (Gorge): As a pre-Christmas contrast, venture south on the A2 Autobahn, taking the Wiener Neustadt exit towards the Schneeberg and passing through Weikersdorf and Willendorf until you reach Wurflach. The 6km trail through the gorge along a rushing— or iced-over—mountain stream is described as "wild romantisch". As an additional seasonal incentive, a Christmas market is opened on certain Advent Sundays. For details, call Tel. 02620 2410 or check the website: gemeinde@wuerflach.at.

Some Magic, Must-See Austrian Sights

The following places are a selection of not-to-be-missed Austrian sites, not only because they are scenically beautiful in and of themselves, but also because they capture vital aspects of the Austrian character. At all seasons of the year, they lend themselves to day- or weekend trips from Vienna.

Kulturwanderweg Baden-Heiligenkreuz-Alland (Lower Austria)

Vienna's environs are not only scenic, they are chock full of history and culture. So it's no wonder that the three townships of Baden, Heiligenkreuz and Alland, just south of the city and easily reached on the A2 Southautobahn (turn off Gießhübel), have put together a narrative "Culture Trail" map (also in English), highlighting points of interest along the way. For example,

- Baden's Beach Baths (Strandbad) with 50 cartloads of sand hauled down from Melk in the 1920s to simulate the Adriatic coast that had once upon a time belonged to Austria;

- Heiligenkreuz's famed Cistercian Abbey founded in the 12th century where you can also hear Gregorian chant performed live by the monks;

- Mayerling, near Alland, where Crown Prince Rudolf and his mistress Mary Vetsera took their lives in the Hapsburg's hunting lodge in January 1889, shocking the world.

The hiking trails are all marked and colour-coded, have huts or "Gasthöfe" along the way and will keep you (and the kids) busy for more than one weekend.

Getting there: From Vienna, take the A2 Southautobahn and exit at Baden, then circle back up towards Vienna.

Note: Request the brochure "Culture Trail: Nature-People-History" from the Austrian Tourist Office

Mariazell (Lower Austria)

In the 12th century, a Benedictine monk named Magnus was trudging through the forest looking for a place to build a monastery. When, at one point, his path was blocked by a huge boulder, Magnus knelt in prayer and asked the Virgin Mary for guidance. Soon the monk heard a great rumbling and the rock split in two, allowing him to pass through. Near the rock, Magnus took a small wooden statue of the Virgin Mary from his knapsack and placed it on a branch. Soon, a small chapel was built to house the statue along with his monastic cell. As word of the miraculous Virgin statue spread across the country, the chapel was enlarged to a church, which itself was expanded to accommodate growing crowds. That was the start of Mariazell.

By 1699, Mariazell received almost 400,000 pilgrims per year, and the faithful began to invoke the Virgin under the title of "Our Lady of Mariazell". Hungarians were amongst the first to make pilgrimages to Mariazell, followed by Croats, Slovakians, Bohemians, Germans and other Central European Catholics. Eventually, Our Lady of Mariazell was given the titles "Great Mother of Austria, Hungary and the Slavic People." Today revered as a national shrine of Austria, Hungary and Bohemia which celebrated its eighth centennial in 1957, Mariazell received Pope John Paul II in 1983 and Pope Benedikt XVI in September 2007.

"Via Sacre" Four-day Pilgrimage: Today's Mariazell is not only picturesque but also a major pilgrimage destination after Rome and Santiago de Compostela (Spain). You can even join the groups of booted or barefooted pilgrims (or bikers) taking the four-day trek from Perchtoldsdorf, on the southern fringe of Vienna. Here, in brief, is their scenic route via the 110-km long Vienna Pilgrimage Route 06, where pilgrims ascend over 3,000m altitude altogether and descend 2,500m. Up and down and up and down, very like life itself, it encourages one to reflect upon life's meaning.

- Day 1: Perchtoldsdorf-Heiligenkreuz-Mayerling-Altenmarkt through hilly pine forests south of Vienna;
- Day 2: Altenmarkt-Hocheck, Kiedneck-Rohr im Gebirge;
- Day 3: Rohr-Kalte Kuchl-St Aegyd am Neuwalde;
- Day 4: St Aegyd-Kernhof Gescheid-Hubertussee-Mariazell.

For accommodation details, please contact www.wallfahrerwirte.at.

Melk (Lower Austria)

Highlighting the apogee of Baroque architecture in Austria, the historic Benedictine Abbey of Melk is one of the world's most famous monastic sites. Located on a rocky outcropping about 50m above the town and overlooking the river Danube, it enjoys the rare distinction of surviving as an active Benedictine monastery continuously since its foundation in 1089 when Leopold II, Margrave of Austria gave one of his castles to Benedictine monks from Lambach Abbey. A school was founded there in the 12th Century, and the monastic library soon became renowned for its extensive manuscript collection. In the 15th Century the abbey became the centre of the Melk Reform movement which reinvigorated the monastic life of Austria and Southern Germany.

Today's impressive structure was erected between 1702 and 1736 by the renowned architect Jakob Prandtauer. Due to its fame and academic stature, Melk escaped dissolution under Emperor Joseph II when many other Austrian abbeys were seized and dissolved between 1780 and 1790. It also managed to survive other threats to its existence during the Napoleonic Wars and in the period following the Nazi Anschluss (takeover) of Austria in 1938, when the school and a large part of the abbey were confiscated by the State. The school was returned to the abbey after the Second World War and now caters for nearly 900 co-ed pupils.

As a tribute to the abbey and its famous library, Umberto Eco named one of the protagonists in his well-known novel, *The Name of the Rose,* „Adso von Melk".

Tours: Visitors can tour Melk Abbey year round, parking in the town and following signs along the Stiftsweg (26). Sights include the main courtyard, abbey church, imperial staircase, marble hall, terrace. and overwhelmingly impressive library. ***Note:*** This visit is also included in the "Kombi-ticket" to the Wachau and Schallaburg mentioned earlier.

Summer Solstice in the Wachau

June 21st and we're in the Wachau to celebrate the summer solstice in the charming company of the *"Kaiserin Elisabeth"*—the boat, that is! Since this delightful "happening" is sold out months in advance, the first time we found it difficult (and not inexpensive) to get tickets; then we had to defend our places against double-booked tour groups—but now we know the secret and we're sharing it with you!

Insider Tip: Book one of only 450 places (€31pp from/to Vienna) on the MS Admiral Tegetthoff that leaves the DDSG Reichsbrücke quai in Vienna at 0800 in the morning, "leave the driving to them" and arrive relaxed at 1430 in Dürnstein. Have a late lunch at the five-star Schloss Restaurant Dürnstein; spend the afternoon exploring the quaint village and castle ruins where Richard, the Lion-hearted was held prisoner in the 12th century. Then try your luck for "last minute" deck chairs (€40pp) or pull out your pre-paid (ca. €60pp) "Sonnwendfeier" ticket and board your boat in Dürnstein for a 1945 departure to ring in the shortest night of the year.

Steam upstream past the town's landmark blue rococo church and sheer rock-climbing walls (Klettergärten) interspersed with mini-vineyards perched at the most precarious angles. Watch the sun play peek-a-boo with the clouds, feel the light wind wafting though the Danube's surface stays smooth as dark blue glass into which your prow slices. Sip your champagne and let the excitement mount at the prospect of what is to come.

Glide past Weissenkirchen as the sun sinks behind hilled vineyards. Gaze across at the opposite bank to see the crowds of people already lining the shores, spreading out picnics, setting up camping tents to celebrate *en famille* and lighting campfires and bonfires, too. The river will be more crowded than you've ever seen it—besides 20 or more big excursion boats all plying their way up upstream to Spitz, there'll be dozens of smaller ones, including private motor boats roaring by, bouncing on the waves churned up by those before them. Everybody's likely to be waving and shouting good cheer.

Now as the river bends gently to the left, the steeple of St Michael's church will come into view. The burgeoning crowds on the shore will make you glad you came by boat. As you approach the famed "Tausend-Eimer Berg" (thousand-bucket mountain) that gives the Wachau its specially named *Steinfeder, Federspiel* and *Smaragd* white wines, every square meter of the north bank of the Danube will be covered with vineyards. From the boat, everything will glide by before your eyes, a silent, slow-motion film.

As you listen to the music and multiple accents all around and look up at the darkening sky, perhaps you'll see the moon and be reminded that, in pagan times, marriages were often performed at this time. June's moon was often called the "honey moon" in reference to the fermented honey mead used in wedding celebrations. Recall the magic of the summer solstice in Shakespeare's "Midsummer Night's Dream" when humans and faeries had star-crossed, love-crossed adventures all night long!

Towards ten at night you'll arrive together with all the other festively-lit boats that gather in front of the village of Spitz with its Hinterhaus Ruin etched on the horizon. All at once, the ruin's entire silhouette will be illuminated with golden torches and then a silver "light waterfall" will spill over from the keep. Fireworks will start going off in all directions, splashing the heavens full of dazzling light while multiple bonfires will give the sky a crimson glow. The Druids viewed midsummer as the wedding of Heaven and Earth and, looking over at the Tausend-Eimer Berg, you'll be moved to see row upon row of golden torchlights being carried by the locals, invisible at night, so that it looks like a procession of glowing ghosts making their way through the darkened vineyards. People may break into spontaneous applause at this sight.

As you glide downstream in darkness, making your way back, every village along the way will outdo itself with its own fireworks. At Dürnstein, a bus will leave to bring you back to Vienna. It may be after midnight before you're home but likely still bright with the excitement of this Summer Solstice in the Wachau!

Note: Organizers do *not* provide re-imbursement due to inclement weather.

For more details, please contact:

DDSG Blue Danube Schiffahrt GmbH - or -
Tel. „+43 1 588 80".
Email: info@ddsg-blue-danube.at
Website: www.ddsg-blue-danube.at

Brandner Schiffahrt
Tel. +0143 7433 25 900
Email:schiffahrt@brandner.at
Website: www.brandner.at

Salzburg (Salzburg province)

One could easily write an entire book just about Salzburg, Austria's fourth largest city and current provincial capital, but we will capture the highlights while pointing you to more detailed accounts.

Suffice it to say here that Salzburg was first a Celtic camp, later a Roman colony, and later still a powerful Archbishopric of the Catholic Church.

Today's "Old Town" with its world famous baroque architecture is one of the best-preserved city centers in the German-speaking world, and was listed as a UNESCO World Heritage Site in 1997. Besides being famous for its alpine setting, Salzburg is also the birthplace of Mozart and the setting for parts of the musical and film *The Sound of Music*.

Salzburg has become an all-time, all-season favorite for tourists, who vastly outnumber locals during peak seasons. In addition to Mozart's birthplace and residence, other notable places include: the entire (mostly pedestrian Old Town with its picturesque Getreidegasse, Salzburg Cathedral and the fortress Hohensalzburg (one of the largest castles in Europe), the Franciscan's Church and St.Peter's cemetery, the Benedictine Nonnberg Abbey, the Mirabell Palace and Gardens and the former Prince-Archbishop's "Residenz" Palace.

And, of course, Salzburg is not only on the frontier to Germany, it is also the portal to the famed Salzkammergut. The world-famous Salzburg Music Festival attracts thousands of visitors during the months of July and August each year.

Getting there: Drive straight out the A1 Westautobahn from Vienna and you'll arrive in Salzburg after about three hours of very scenic driving. Or take any of the frequent trains from the Westbahnhof, Of course, if you're in a hurry, you can always fly; AUA has multiple flights each day, but it's almost a shame to miss the gorgeous scenery!

Hallstatt (Upper Austria)

Idyllic Hallstatt, tucked away on a steep Salzkammergut mountainside just above its namesake lake, is in fact one of the prehistoric cradles of Western civilization and honoured by being named both one of the world's most beautiful villages and also a UNESCO cultural heritage site.

Once precious salt has been mined here since the Neolithic Age when settlers built their dwellings on stilts in the fjord-deep lake. Today, although the town's population barely exceeds 1,000, in season it is overwhelmed by tourists. The best trick is to come pre-season for the Corpus Christi boat procession on the lake, take the cable car up to the **salt mines**, or stay overnight when the town settles down to its sleepy romantic self. See vignette in Section 4 for more details.

Getting there: Easiest is to take your car, driving west from Vienna on the A1 Westautobahn and exit at Gmunden am Traunsee, following the signs along Hwy 145 to Bad Ischl and from there continue south through Bad Goisern and follow the signs to Hallstatt. You can either park at the entrance to the village or across the lake and take the ferry boat over.

Websites: http://en.wikipedia.org/wiki/Hallstatt,

http://europeforvisitors.com/switzaustria/articles/hallstatt.htm

Kitzbhühel (Tyrol)

Kitzbühel, one of the oldest—and most exclusive—holiday resorts in the Austrian Alps, was settled in prehistoric times and developed thanks to its copper deposits and favourable location along the route from Venice to Munich. Already chartered as a town by 1271, Kitzbühel continued to flourish and was fortunate to have never suffered war or invasion.

If "invaded" now, it's only by well-intentioned (and usually well-heeled) tourists from near and far who come to revel in the exquisite alpine scenery, the swimming, riding and golf in summer and the skiing and *après ski* in winter.

Speaking of winter sports, Kitzbühel is the Mecca of the Modern Downhill! The Hahnenkamm Men's Downhill—with its breathtaking Streif (the "streak" with 85% incline at its steepest point and speeds of up to 140km/hr)—each year in January bring thousands of high-spirited spectators to "Kitz". There's also winter polo—on snow no less—plus cross-country skiing, sleigh rides and you-name-it.

Kitz is very *avant-garde* and tourism-friendly. For information, contact Kitzbühel Tourism, Hinterstadt 18, A-6370 Kitzbühel and/or http://www.ifyouski.com/Resorts/View/?objectid=449004

Getting there: It's about a 4.5-hour drive southwest of Vienna, first on the A1 Westautobahn and then past Salzburg and across the "little German corner" past Lofer and St Johann in Tirol on B161, which connects Kitzbühel with Mittersill (B161) and Wörgl. (B 170). You can also travel directly and daily by train from Vienna to Kitzbühel.

Zell am See (Salzburg)

Zell am See is, along with Kitzbühel, one of the oldest and most scenic settlements in Austria, founded by the Romans on the banks of the Zeller Lake, which reflects the glacier-capped peaks in its pristine blue waters. This region, called the Pinzgau, offers endless sports opportunities year 'round, including one of Europe's most popular airports for sport flying and gliding. See Section 4, *"Autumn in the Mountains"* for more details.

Getting there: Besides direct train connections right into the heart of the town, you can also take the scenic drive, continuing on from Kitzbühel on Highway 161 that crosses Pass Thurn, with its spectacular views of the High Austrian Alps (Hohe Tauern) to Mittersill. Then continue along the Salzach Valley until you reach Zell.

Weblinks: Europa-Sportregion Zell am See-Kaprun: http://www. europasportregion.info.

Zell am See, Oberpinzgau, Salzburger Land: http://www.oberpinzgau. de/Highlights/zell_am_see.htm

Großglockner Road

This stunning high alpine highway—a marvel of engineering completed in 1935—takes you from Bruck, just a few kilometres from Zell am See, through the spartan-looking Fuschertal past the Bear Gorge (Bärenschlucht) and up, up, up until it begins to open out with a panoramic view of the Sonnenwelleck peaks. Keep going (down shift and take a deep breath of the crisp mountain air!) and at last, after passing by the "Witches' Kitchen" with its eerie wisps of smoke-like fog, you will arrive at the high point—the Hochtor (2,505m/8,448ft) where you have a splendid view to the Pasterze Glacier and the Großglockner, Austria's highest peak (3,798m/12,458ft), the top of Austria's world!

Franz-Josefs-Höhe is the starting point for all sorts of summer hiking and climbing tours. The "Glacier Road" ends here with a spacious panorama terrace, restaurants, shops and, at the end of Panorama Path, a free observation point where you may spy climbers making their way like tiny ants up the vast Pasterze Glacier towards the Adlersruhe hut.

Descending the other side, we're now in Carinthia and, after more zik-zak curves, you reach the Kasereck, where spicy mountain cheese is produced, and then—all of a sudden—you see a spire.

Heiligenblut (Carinthia)

A lone, slender, stone spike juts into the clear blue sky, man's attempt to capture the solitary grandeur of the Großglockner in the background. The church of **Heiligenblut** (meaning *holy blood*) greets us.

Situated high in the Mölltal valley at 1,288 meters, Heiligenblutat is one of the most scenic villages of Austria. Its 15th century Gothic pilgrimage church of Saint Vinzenz allegedly contains a <u>relic</u> of Christ's Holy Blood. brought in 1496 from Constantinople. The cemetery has a bronze-paged book listing the names of mountaineers who left their lives on the Großglockner and nearby.

Other attractions include the Heiligenblut-Schareck cable car (2,606 m) with its panorama view, an open-air museum, a number of waterfalls and lakes. The construction of the nearby railway tunnel to the Fleißalm mountain area (1,798 m) is unique in Europe in that the 1.6km long tunnel is filled with water in summer but serves as a railway tunnel to the Fleißalm winter sports region in winter.

St. Veit and the Trigonale (Carinthia)

It is obvious from the sumptuous architecture and spacious town square that St Veit an der Glan is a special place. In fact, before Klagenfurt upstaged it in the 16th century, St Veit was the seat of the dukes of Carinthia. The city walls are mostly intact, the town centre is flush with flowers, and the late Gothic town hall with its three storey Renaissance courtyard enhanced with sgraffiti arcades is an impressive tribute to St Veit's former position of power and culture.

Today it's the culture that draws crowds each summer: in particular, the unique "Trigonale" three-week long (mid-June through early July) Festival of Early Music staged at three Carinthian sites—St Veit, Maria Saal and St Georgen am Längsee. Visit all three: with a 25-km radius, each has its own speical atmosphere. Just as a sampler, on the evening we attended, the group Harmonia Caelestis was performing—five highly talented young musicians: the leader and cembalo/organ player hailed from Malaysia; the lutist/guitarist from Norway; the (female) baroque violin, viola from Germany; the mute cornet player/zink from Wales; and the (female) bass gamba/diskant violin player from Ireland. What an exquisite mixture! Prices run from €25-50pp and tickets can be pre-ordered through the Trigonale Box Office at Tel. +43 (0) 463 500 360 or karten@trigonale.com. Enthusiasts can also sponsor this relatively new initiative (2002) and receive a number of benefits. Check the website at: www.trigonale.com.

Lech am Arlberg (Voralberg)

Lech/Oberlech am Arlberg (1,440m/1,700m) is a tiny linked mountain village with some 2,000 local population that nevertheless plays perfect host to the world's jet set and royalty.

In winter, a ski—and *après ski*—resort *non plus ultra*, you can connect via cable cars and ski lifts with the well-groomed pistes of neighbouring Zürs and St. Anton, all part of the greater Arlberg Ski Circus. Lech is also home to "Der Weisse Ring" or "The White Ring" which is a rough circle of runs and lifts that conduct a tour around the area. This circle extends quite high into the snow-capped mountains where you can also go heli-skiing and ski-touring.

Not to be outdone, summer also features a diversity of high-alpine sports activities, from hiking to mountain-biking, climbing to swimming, golf and tennis to fishing, paragliding to canyoning and rafting. Whatever you can think of, they'll offer it!

Getting there: One of the most stress-less ways is by ÖBB "Wedelweiss" overnight train from Vienna that lets you alight at early morning light on the Arlberg, includes train, transfer and ski pass, and takes you overnight back home as well. Better than bucking that long 8-10 hour drive, especially in winter!

Website: http://www.oebb.at/vip8/pv/de/Pressecorner/ Presseinformationen/05-12-12_Wedelweiss.

Crossing Borders: Austria's Near Neighbours

Slovakia: Bratislava

With a population of some 450,000, Bratislava (formerly called Pressburg) is Slovakis's capital and largest city, as well as the political, cultural and economic centre of the country since it became independent of Czechoslovakia and the former Soviet Union during the "Velvet Revolution" of 1993.

Situated in southwestern Slovakia, Bratislava is the only national capital in the world that borders two countries: Austria and Hungary. The impressive **Bratislava Castle** dominates the skyline above the Danube.

Over the past decade the city has had a welcome "face lift" and now boasts a pleasant pedestrian shopping zone featuring crystal and handcrafts shops, as well as restaurants and spacious squares.

Less than two hours from Vienna, it's easy to take a day trip to Bratislava by car or train or even bike. Don't forget your passport though! Nicest in summer is to hop aboard the Twin Cities Liner Hydrofoil that transports you in only 75 minutes from "heart to heart"—that is, Vienna's city center at the Schwedenplatz to Bratislava's Razusovo Nabrezie Embankment just across from the hotels Danube and Devin. The catamaran hydrofoil operates daily, several times per day, in season and tickets (€15-€27) are bookable online at the Twin City Liner website. http://www.twincityliner.com/.

Hungary: Sopron

Just southeast of Vienna lies Hungary and, ever since the lifting of the Iron Curtain, it's only a tempting few hours away. Take a day trip to visit the historic city of Sopron. Populated by rows of historical houses, it is still surrounded by the remnants of a horseshoe shaped fortress wall dating from Roman times when they called the settlement "Scarbantia".

This medieval city, formerly called Ödenburg, is situated at the Amber Road and still has the richest collection of historic buildings in Hungary. Main attractions include the "Fire Tower", the City Hall with its historic exhibit, two medieval synagogues and St. Mary's Church, dating from 1280, where three queens were crowned. Though badly bombed in World War II, many relics from the Middle Ages have survived. Ongoing reconstruction makes this a stunning trip back in time.

Hungarians refer to Sopron as the "The Most Loyal City" since it voted in a 1921 referendum to remain part of Hungary rather than join Austria as the province of Burgenland did.

In August 1989 Sopron was the site of the "Pan-European Picnic", a protest by anti-communist activists on the Austrio-Hungarian border. Over 200 East German citizens illegally crossed the border here, helping pave the way for the mass flight of East German that culminated in the fall of the Berlin Wall in November 1989.

Today it's less about escaping oppression than discovering opportunities: everything from picture framing to plastic surgery and dental implants can be had here for a fraction of the price in Austria. For more details, please consult: http://wikitravel.org/en/Sopron.

Hungary: Budapest

Budapest, the capital of Hungary with about 1.7 million population, is the country's principal political, cultural, commercial, industrial and transportation center. Its Roman origins parallelled those of Vienna but in the 10th century, the area came under the domination of Magyars from Central Asia who founded the Kingdom of Hungary soon after. An autonomous Hungarian government was finally established under the Austro-Hungarian Ausgleich („Compromise") of 1867.

Many civilian lives and buildings were lost in Budapest towards the end of World War II. Between 20-40% of the city's 250,000 Jewish inhabitants died through Nazi and Arrow Cross genocide in 1944-45. Despite this, Budapest today has the highest number of Jewish citizens per capita of any European city.

Today's Budapest is a shopping mecca with Váci Utca, the main shopping street, catering to tourists. Budapest has the most shopping centers in Europe, including WestEnd City Center, the largest shopping centre in Central and Eastern Europe until just recently, and the biggest Tesco and Auchan hypermarkets in the world. The Great Market Hall is a large indoor market and a major tourist attraction. All luxurious brands can be found, on the high streets, such as Andrássy Avenue and Váci utca.

Transportation: All major roads lead to/leave from Budapest. Budapest is also a major railway terminus and several daily trains go back and forth to/from Vienna. For details in English, please see http://www.oebb.at/vip8/oebb/en/. Budapest Ferihegy International Airport has three passenger terminals: Ferihegy 1 tends to serve the many discount airlines now flying to and from Budapest. Malév (Hungarian Airlines) began to upgrade its fleet in 2003 and by 2005 allegedly owned the most modern fleet in Europe.

Within the city, public transport is mainly provided by BKV, which operates buses, trolleys, trams, suburban railway lines, the metro, boats and many other special vehicles. Budapest's tramline is the busiest traditional city tram line in the world, with 50-metre long trains running at 60 to 90 second intervals at peak time and usually packed with people. Night traffic service is outstandingly good.

The Danube flows through the middle of Budapest on its way to the Black Sea. The river is easily navigable and so Budapest has historically been a major commercial port. In the summer months a scheduled hydrofoil service operates, allowing passengers to pass through three capitals on the banks of the Danube—Budapest, Bratislava and Vienna—in only six hours. Please see http://www.vienna-hydrofoil.hotels-in-budapest-hungary.com/index.html?gclid=CNTb3ui-94wCFQYMXgodKEEM9 for details.

Czech Republic: Prague

Prague—widely considered to be one of the most beautiful cities in Europe— is the capital and largest city of the Czech Republic. Situated on the Vltava River in central Bohemia, it has been the political, cultural and economic center of the Czech state for over 1,000 years. The city proper is home to nearly 1.2 million people, while its greater metropolitan area counts an estimated 1.9 million people. Prague is one of Europe's most visited cities and its historic centre was named a UNESCO World Heritage Site in 1992. Epithets for Prague include "the golden city" and "city of a hundred spires".

Today's Prague was settled in the Paleolithic Age and served as a nexus on land and river trade routes between southern and northern parts of Europe. By the early 10th century, the area around Prague Castle had developed into an important trading centre, where merchants from all over Europe gathered. In 973, a bishopric was founded in Bohemia with the bishop's palace located on the Prague castle grounds. The Middle Ages and beyond saw Prague continue to gain in importance and respect throughout Europe. Later Bohemia and Moravia were subsumed into the Hapsburg Empire and Prague was second to Vienna until after the First World War.

World War I ended with the defeat of the Austro-Hungarian Empire and the creation of Czechoslovakia. Prague was chosen as its capital. For most of its history Prague had been an ethnically mixed city with important Czech, German and Jewish populations. From 1939, when the country was occupied by Nazi Germany, and during World War II most Jews either fled the city or were killed in the Holocaust. The ethnic German population also either fled or was expelled in the months after May 1945. During the gathering and transfer of Germans a number of local massacres occurred resulting in an unknown number of fatalities.

After the war, Prague again became the capital of Czechoslovakia but the country remained under strong Russian political influence. In February 1948, Prague became the centre of a communist coup. In 1967 Alexander Dubček proclaimed a new phase in the country's life, beginning with the short-lived "Prague Spring", which aimed at a democratic reform of institutions. The Soviet Union and the rest of the Warsaw Pact reacted, occupying Czechoslovakia and the capital in August 1968, suppressing any attempt at innovation under the treads of their tanks.

In 1989, after the Berlin Wall had fallen, and the Velvet Revolution crowded the streets of Prague, Czechoslovakia finally freed itself from communism and Soviet influence, and Prague benefited deeply from the new mood. In 1993, after the split of Czechoslovakia, Prague became the capital city of the new Czech Republic.

Since the fall of the Iron Curtain, Prague has become one of Europe's (and the world's) most popular tourist destinations. It is the sixth most visited European city after London, Paris, Rome, Madrid and Berlin. Located about five hours from Vienna by car, the quickest access is by plane.

4. A YEAR OF SEASONS: AUSTRIAN VIGNETTES AND LOCAL RECIPES

Austria's not only about the past. It's also a contemporary Shangri-la for all seasons! So this section will treat you to a series of vignettes—let's call them "Austrian aperitifs"—to whet your appetite for slightly off-the-beaten-track experiences that you can do yourself, either alone or with friends and family. Each vignette captures unique features of Austria's different provinces during all four seasons of the year. And, as a culinary plus, the vignettes feature local wines and recipes you can reproduce at home. We hope you enjoy this "interactive" part of *Exploring Austria: Vienna and Beyond.*

Let's start witih a small buffet and a festive toast!

❖ **Austrian Aperitifs: A Toast!**

Schlumberger Sekt, made in the classical *Méthode Champenoise* is the perfect Austrian aperitif!

2004 Dom Sekt	2005 Schilcher Sekt Rosé
2001 Chardonnay Brut	2004 Pomino Bianco
2002 Privatkeller Cabernet/Merlot	

Rustic Cold Buffet à la Schlumberger

Mozzarella with tomatoes, avocadoes and fresh basil
Marinated *Tafelspitz* with Styrian pumpkin oil
Chicken breast with Waldorf salad
White asparagus with vinaigrette
Melon with proscuitto

"Sekt": Secrets of the Perfect "Austrian Aperitif"
Weine von höchster Bekömmlichkeit— Salubrious Sekt

Dry, sparkling "Sekt"—the embodiment of the perfect "Austrian Aperitif." Effervescent and refreshing, Sekt takes two-three labour-intensive years to produce. In the top houses, "Sekt" is identical to "champagne" in terms of production methods; however, the French placed the term "champagne" under copyright in 1919 so that it can only be applied to products from that specific geographic region of northern France.

Never mind. Burgenland and Bad Vöslau bei Wien became Austria's Champagne region so that, to this day, good Austrian Sekt is made identically to French champagne!

Let's start at the beginning—and it all begins in the vineyards with the "right" grapes and the best care and fervent prayers for perfect weather, too—mild, sunny, sparse rain in August. Austria's best "Sekt grapes" are the Welsch Riesling, Grüner Veltliner, White Burgundy and Chardonnay, mostly from its easternmost province of Burgenland around the Neusiedlersee. These grapes are hand-harvested and combined to form a *Cuvée.* Then a special patented champagne yeast is introduced to transform the natural sugar into alcohol and carbon dioxide bubbles. Now the wine is bottled and, using the "traditional method," a very complex process ensues in which everything must be meticulously monitored and controlled for 18-24 months.

Visiting *Schlumberger* in the Heiligenstadt suburb of Vienna, we experience this process first-hand as we are shown through its 2.2 km of 300-year-old "caves"—a labyrinth of brick, high-vaulted ceilings that ensure stable year-round temperatures of 11-13°C with 80-90% humidity.

It's a bit overwhelming actually to be in the august company of 200,000 bottles of *sekt in spé*—row upon row, corridor upon corridor—like élèves on their way to becoming prima ballerinas!

For that, one needs sparkle! And the fine, spritely bubbles that give Sekt its "sparkling" character come in part from the champagne yeast that intensies the fermentation process; in part from the labour-intensive "rütteln und schütteln"—the "laying on of hands" and turning of bottles 1/8 of a turn each day for 25 consecutive days! Then they are stored at ever steeper angles in the row upon row wine racks in the cool semi-darkness of the caves. As a finale, they are turned 24 times and stored at a steep 70° angle for their final transformation. A symbolic chrysalis.

Twenty-four months of "TLC" (tender loving care) is terminated by a rather abrupt procedure when the top of the bottle, now stored vertically upside down, is quickly cooled to –25°C (!), the temporary cork is removed and the yeast is virtually cold-catapulted out of the bottle.

Then the wine bottles march single file, stiffly as wooden soldiers in the *Nutcracker Suite* but rattling their dark green glass sabres, onto a conveyor belt that will send them to be definitively wire-corked, spruced up with etiquettes and finally neatly packed into boxes. Voilá! Austrian "champagne," 15% of which is exported to 16 different countries.

The Schlumberger Sekt "debutante," on the scene since 2004, is the "Dom," named after the Austria's Salzburger Dom. A combination of 2/3 chardonnay and 1/3 pinot noir grapes, with its noble bouquet, fine-pearled *mousseux* and light but unmistakable flavour, it aspires to be Austria's newest "cult wine." Try it. You'll see why!

Schlumberger Wine and Sekt Cellars **Heiligenstädterstr. 43, A-1190 Vienna, Austria**

Tel. +43 1 368 60 38-0 **Website: www.schlumberger.at**

Schlumberger, Austria's oldest and noblest sparkling wine producer, headquartered in Vienna and nearby Bad Vöslau, also has a fascinating history. Its founder, Robert Schlumberger, loved champagne so much that he even went to work in France's Ruinart Père & Fils in Reims. Then he fell in love with the Viennese Sophie Kirchner, married, moved to Austria and founded his own company in 1842—in the heyday of the Hapsburg Empire—and brought his *champagne* expertise with him.

It wasn't long before his "Sparkling Vöslauer" was the "in" aperitif of *fin de siècle* Viennese society. And as aristocratic titles were also a very "in" thing at the time, Robert became Imperial and Royal Purveyor to the Court and soon bore the title of "Edler von Goldeck."

Today **Dom Sekt** is Austria's newest "cult wine." Described as "mystical, extravagant and exclusive," it's a combination of "wisdom, philosophy and intuition." Three Austrians have created it: Manfred Tenant from the "green heart" of southern Styria, F.X. Pichler from the world-famous Wachau, and Illa Szemes, whose very name recalls Austria's fiery Hungarian heritage.

Schlumberger continues to expand its pivotal position in the Austrian Sekt industry through a combination of *avant garde* technical knowledge and *Einfühlungsvermögen*—that subtle intuitive sense that transforms tradition and knowledge into 'wisdom'—not only in this, but every sphere of life. As they put it:

> *"Die Glut bewahren und nicht die Asche hüten."*
> **Fan the embers, not the ashes.**

In terms of Austria and its New World aperitifs, that means: be innovative, take risks (albeit carefully calculated ones) and create a new future out of a rich past. An *aperitif* is just the beginning!

Intro to the Salzkammergut: Scenic Treasure Chest between Mountains and Lakes

What is it anyway, this almost unpronounceable „Salzkammergut"? Well, to start with, it's a 60 x 60 sq km geographic region rooted in history and located within the Austrian provinces of Upper Austria, Salzburg and Styria. Alpine summits encircle almost 80 pristine lakes and are reflected in their still, crystal-clear waters. Stunning beauty abounds.

So did early civilizations. The first evidence of prehistoric cultures in this area was the Mondsee culture (2,800-1,800 BC) with lake dwellings built on stilts, followed by others that gave rise to the archeological term Hallstatt Period (800-400 BC).

Later, in the Middle Ages, the salt mines made this region highly valuable to its rulers. After the Hapburgs came to power in the 13th century, they created the Salzkammergut (literally "Imperial Salt Chamber"), the authority charged with running the precious salt mines that covered an area stretching from Gmunden in the northwest to Aussee in the southeast. And later still, in the 19-20th century, it was the next-to-last Hapsburg Emperor Franz Josef who spent all of his 83 summers in Bad Ischl that put the Salzkammergut unequivocally on Europe's power map.

Still, for the first several hundred years, the only people besides the indigenous population allowed entrance were those engaged in salt-trading on behalf of the Imperial Hapsburg family. So the beauties of the Salzkammergut were long a closely guarded secret—a small paradise in the heart of the Empire that would not be discovered and opened to outside visitors until the 19th century.

Emerging from obscurity at the height of Vienna's *fin-de-siècle* glamour as a magnet for Europe's creative geniuses, the Salzkammergut became Vienna's summer escape, its spiritual countryside ("Seelenlandschaft") or, as author Dietmar Grieser puts it in his *Nachsommertraum im Salzkammergut,* Vienna's artistic *dependence.* Along with the capital's upper crust, some of the first—and most famous—to frequent this European Shangri-la were from the arts scene. Here in *locus genii,* artists found their inspiration. The list is long and continues to this day, but below are a few of the more memorable figures for whom the Salzkammergut acted as something of an artistic aphrodisiac.

Writers, Musicians and Artists Inspired by the Salzkammergut

Adalbert Stifter am Hallstättersee (1845): Receptive for a story and hiking around the Dachstein with geologist, alpine expert and friend, Friedrich Simony, poet Stifter was inspired on the spot by a chance meeting with two cherubic alpine children caught in a storm while picking wild straw-berries and, later, by his first encounter with the Dachstein ice caves. The result is "Bergkristall" (Mountain Crystal), one of the world's most moving Christmas stories. Others followed. Simony's own character, as reflected in his "Night on the Dachstein Summit," found itself later imbedded in Stifter's best known work, "Nachsommer" (Indian Summer).

Wagner's muse, Mathilde von Wesendonk, am Traunsee (1878-1902): Granted, the great Wagner himself was never here ... but his musical influence was, enhanced through the untiring efforts of Mathilde, wife of a wealthy German industrialist, for whom Wagner was practically a god and her imposing Villa Traunblick a virtual Temple. It is said that theirs was the passionate yet pristine relationship that inspired Wagner's "Tristan and Isolde."

Gustav Mahler am Attersee (1893-1896): Mahler spent four highly creative summers in Steinbach am Attersee where his tiny Music Pavilion served as the "vacation composer's" sanctuary, providing the peace and quiet to work in a picturesque setting that also suited his pocketbook. "Interruptions forbidden on pain of Death" was the draconian rule that allowed him to complete most of his Second and all of his Third Symphony, the latter titled "A Summer Morning Dream" that transformed the Salzkammergut's scenic magic into music.

Theodore Billroth am Wolfgangsee (1883-1893): An all-round Renaissance man, Prussian-born Billroth, an amateur pianist good enough to accompany Swedish Nightingale Jenny Lind and later a close friend of Johannes Brahms, moved to Vienna to become a world-renowned surgeon. Finding the perfect spot in St. Gilgen, he became an amateur architect and oversaw the construction of a large summer villa where his family felt "more at home than all the months in Vienna." Today the site of a four-star hotel, it still bears his name.

August Strindberg am Mondsee (1893): Eccentric, Swedish playwright Strindberg was married for a short time to (equally eccentric) Austrian journalist Frida Uhl whose family's imposing villa overlooked the Mondsee. Invited by his mother-in-law to "come and stay as long as you like," Strindberg came but spent only a few paranoid, catastrophic days when his bride refused to join him, his father-in-law threw him out, and he fantasized about "Death in the Mondsee."

Gustav Klimt am Attersee (1900-1916): Klimt spent 16 consecutive summers on the Attersee in the company of the Flöge clan whose couture-designer, Emilie Flöge, was his mistress, muse and model for the world famous portrait,"The Kiss." Klimt also painted landscapes around his Oleander Villa, Schloß Kammer and flower-strewn meadows and orchards, near and far, viewed in foreshortening through his telescope.

In 1997 UNESCO designated the Salzkammergut as one of its World Heritage Sites with the following description: *"Human activity in the magnificent natural landscape of the Salzkammergut began in prehistoric times, with the salt deposits being exploited as early as the 2nd millennium BC. This resource formed the basis of the area's prosperity up to the middle of the 20th century, a prosperity that is reflected in the fine architecture of the town of Hallstatt, one of the most photographed villages in all of Europe."* Today the Salzkammergut with its 76 mountain-encircled lakes and scenic alpine beauty is a "paradise found" for visitors from all over the world. The following vignettes should whet your appetite; after all, there's far more here than just salt!

SUMMER IN THE SALZKAMMERGUT: PARADISE FOUND!

JUNE: Heaven's Gate: Ballooning In The Salzkammergut

Über den Wolken muß die Freiheit wohl grenzenlos sein ..."

"Above the clouds, there must be boundless freedom ..."
- Reinhard Mey (Austrian singer/composer)

"Lots of people *fantasize* about boundless freedom. We *experience* it—ballooning!"

Experiencing first-hand is what I want too, not just looking up at these graceful balloons from the ground. And that "live it yourself" motto is what leads me to the St. Wolfgang Balloon and Airship Company and its exuberant owner, Austrian Helmut Tucek. His team is there to facilitate that feeling of freedom while floating high above one of the most scenic sites on earth, Austria's Salzkammergut, a summer and winter wonderland.

It's a cloudless summer day when I first stop by their hanger close to Strobl on the Wolfgangsee to inquire. The sign on the gate says, *"90% of what we work with is just hot air!"* I like this guy's sense of humour even before I meet him. Then he comes along and that does the trick: that classic blond charm and wit that makes Austrian men a success at everything from ski instructing to operetta singing. I ask him how he got started in the ballooning business.

"My first encounter with ballooning was in a children's story-book," Helmut says, "but it took twenty more *years* before I actually got the chance to try it. And then about twenty *seconds* before I was hooked for life! How true it is, as the philosophers say, that the *journey itself* is the goal. You have to *experience* every bit of it—the sights, smells, sounds and the soaring sensation that is ballooning. It's addictive! By the way, I'm also addicted to free-fall parachuting—I sky dive from the balloon and take people tandem. Want to try it sometime?"

"Absolutely, but for now let's just take one fright—er, flight—at a time, OK?"

Helmut and his team of pilots and ground coordinators started their company back in 1992 and have been luring adventurers ever since. Looks like I'm the next. So, to be close to the action, I decide to stay in Strobl. After checking into the Seehotel Lilly, I'm off for a late afternoon stroll along the lakefront, which is where I'm sitting, soaking up the Indian Summer sun, when my mobile phone rings at the 1900 appointed time. It's the balloon base announcing, *"Es wird klappen. Morgen soll ein Pracht Tag werden!"* "It's going to work. Tomorrow should be a fantastic day!"

I'm awakened at 0600, not by my alarm, but by the bells in the Baroque tower of Strobl's parish church just across the way. The moment my eyes pop open, they veer towards the window to check the weather: Ahhh! For once the weather report was right! Not a cloud! Just the soft morning fog that veils the water.

Up. Scramble. Don my alpine gear with multiple layers of clothing, cap and gloves stuffed into my pockets. After all, it's early and we'll be up high, I reason, priding myself on my foresight gleaned from years of mountaineering. *Hubris* as it turns out.

Next thing I know, the silence is broken by the rumble of a heavy motor as a big 125 hp Land Rover Defender 1100 approaches, with stowed basket and balloon in tow.

"Grüß Gott, bin der Werner." In a lilting, all but indecipherable local dialect, pilot Werner, ruggedly handsome with his Austrian-blue eyes, salt-and-pepper crew cut and short stubble beard, introduces himself. "Hallo, und ich bin der Dieter," says the sixty-ish driver, light blue eyes twinkling behind his glasses. Into the Land Rover and off we go to the take-off site, a meadow located about 640m above sea level on the Guggenberg overlooking the Mondsee. Meanwhile, Werner is checking the weather once again by mobile phone.

On our short drive to the lift-off site, I learn that he's a licensed pilot and does about 100 of these balloon trips a year. When I ask if he also flies small planes, he says, "No tin crates for me! Not when I can have a wicker basket and balloon!"

As for Dieter, he confides that he was a former body guard for Chancellor Helmut Kohl and other elite German politicians; now he's an avid mountaineer, addicted to the nearby Dachstein where he even does winter ascents with ice picks and crampons. I tell him that was my first-ever mountain. Now there's a bond!

Meanwhile, we arrive at the meeting point and greet the other passengers—we'll be eight today, five men, three women, all Austrians and all on our "maiden voyage." Introducing ourselves, it turns out that Anna, a fit-and-feisty little lady in our midst, is celebrating her 80th birthday today and was given this balloon ride as a surprise present by her family, including great grandchildren, who have come to see her off! She takes it all brightly in stride. For all of us, anticipation runs high.

Now Werner calls us all together and says, "We'll be taking our newest and biggest balloon, the Warsteiner, sponsored by the German brewery; it has a hot air capacity of 7,000 cubic metres. The basket holds ten people—and we're nine, including me—plus four cylinders of propane gas for a total of 320 litres that would be enough to heat a normal-sized house for 2-3 months. The height of the basket and balloon together is 34 metres, as high as a four-story house, when filled … but first, we have to fill it. Luckily, ballooning is a team sport!"

We all pitch in, helping to tip the wicker basket gently out of its trailer and onto the field. Then we heave-ho the balloon bag and unpack what seems like kilometres of lightweight, bright yellow nylon, stretching it in a straight line down the dewy cloverfield. I help cap the top of the balloon with velcro bands while, way off at the other end, Werner and the others are clipping the 28 cables into the eight carabiners that connect the basket to the balloon. Now, we're all ready—except for the hot air on this cool morning.

To solve that problem, Werner positions three propane gas jets and switches on an industrial strength Honda fan to blow hot air into the balloon, the sides of which are held aloft by all eight of us. The gas jets roar and flames blast hot air, like a dragon spewing fire into a quivering nylon eggshell! It works.

The balloon fills quickly, billowing out, and Werner even walks around inside, checking the seams and steering cable. Within minutes the balloon takes on a life of its own, lifts itself off the grass and arches upwards into the morning mist.

Time to get in, before she floats off without us! A scurry of red anoraks and hiking boots, using the rope loops as ladders, we clamber into the basket. There we are, ready to go.

Werner turns on all three jets full-blast. He's sweating now, pulls off his blue anorak with its Balloon and Airship Company insignia and is suddenly all business. Pulling cables, checking gauges, squinting up into the vastness of this yellow balloon that is to whisk us up above the clouds.

Whsss! Whssh! Whssh! The hot jets blast. The balloon stretches skywards. The basket budges, bumps once, twice, then lifts ever so slightly … and starts to glide sideways above the meadow. All at once, soundlessly, effortlessly, we start to ascend as if by magic! All of us awestruck as we rise and the ground recedes, leaving our well-wishers below, no one says a word as we float up, up and away through the early morning mist. Such fragile beauty.

"Balloons can't be *steered*," Werner says. "They can only be *finessed* to float in certain directions, using the wind outside their envelope for direction, the heated air inside to adjust the altitude." We see what he means when we get too close to nearby wooded hills on our ascent and have to descend temporarily to catch a different airstream, before emerging once again from the sea of clouds below into the bright sunshine above.

Ballooning—A Brief History

Ballooning began about 220 years ago in France, pioneered by the Montgolfier brothers, Joseph and Ettienne, whose family was in the paper manufacturing business. The first (likely unwilling) balloonists in history were a sheep, a duck and a rooster sent aloft in a hot air balloon in **1783**.

People followed the same year when a hot air balloon built of paper and silk by the Montgolfier brothers and piloted by two noblemen from the court of Louis XVI and Marie Antoinette ascended 500 feet above the rooftops of Paris for a 22-minute flight that landed them kilometres away in a vineyard. The local farmers were outraged and suspicious of this "fiery dragon descending from the sky" so the pilots offered them champagne to placate them and to celebrate the first manned flight—a tradition that endures to this day.

At its inception, ballooning was a sport only for the "haute volé," literally the high-flyers. The only people who had the leisure time and inclination for such flights of fancy were Europe's titled nobility. So when "commoners" took to the skies, a new practice emerged: after each maiden voyage, the ballooner went through a baptism by fire after which s/he received a title and became an honorary member of the ballooning aristocracy!

*Though initially a pre-revolutionary French pastime, ballooning quickly spread to Italy, then to England and finally to America where it also became a competitive sport. National and inter-national championships were introduced and some noteworthy records set. In August **1932** Swiss scientist Auguste Piccard was the first to achieve a manned flight into the earth's stratosphere, reaching a record altitude of 16,000 metres. Following in his father's footsteps, Bertrand Piccard set both an altitude (11,737m) and distance (40,814km) record in **1999,** circumnavigating the globe in his Breitling Orbiter 3, together with Brian Jones (UK).*

But one needn't be a "profi." Anyone can enjoy the experience as a passenger. Today's balloons have two main technological advantages: they use rip-stop nylon, a very safe and reliable material for the envelope, and liquid propane gas burners to heat the air in the envelope. In Austria today, there are ca. 300 balloons and about a dozen commercial companies. Mine was:

The Balloon and Airship Company
Schwarzenbach 73
A-5360 St. Wolfgang, Austria
Tel. (+43) 06138 3027
Email: willkommen@freiheit.at
Website: www.freiheit.at

Approximate Prices: €280-350,
depending on the number of
passengers, for a flight lasting about
1.5 hours over Austria's scenic
Salzkammergut. The "Transalpine
Express" costs about €1,000 per
person, including a festive overnight
in Italy.

Others Austrian companies include (but are not limited to):

Ballonfahrer Club Österreichischer
A-1230 Wien, Endresstr 79/4

Alpen Ballonfahrten
A-8971 Rohrmoos-Untertal,
Wiesenweg 76

Balloon Exclusive Air
A-2532 Heiligenkreuz, Gruberstr 11

Ballonclub Salzburg
A-5020 Salzburg, Kendlerstr 90

Ballonfahren macht Spass GmbH
A-4400 Steyr, Sierninger Str 80

Ballonteam - Kärnten<
A-9300 Hörzendorf, Nr. 2

Ballooning Tyrol Ballonfahrten u
Freizeitaktivitäten GesmbH
A-6380 St. Johann in Tirol,
Speckbacherstr 33a

Dachstein Tauern-Balloon
A-8972 Ramsau am Dachstein,
Vorberg 165

Drifting in a northeasterly direction, we pass over the village of Zell am Moos on the Irrsee and then into the air traffic space of the Salzburg Airport. Werner contacts the control tower, giving our position and requesting permission to ascend to 2,500m. This granted, he lowers a transponder over the side of the basket so that we will be visible on their radar—after all, a hot air balloon is no match for an airliner! Reassuringly, we see not a single plane the whole morning.

Silence—except for the occasional blast of the propane gas jet that send bright orange flames upwards to heat the air in the balloon's envelope and take us ever higher. Ascending, Austria's snow-covered peaks emerge to greet us. Werner reels off their names: "There's the Schafberg, the Tennengebirge, Hochkönig, Gosaukamm, Dachstein, Großvenediger and the Großglockner, Austria's highest peak at 3,798m. And closer by are some Salzkammergut lakes: the Mondsee, Fuschlsee, Attersee, still a little in the clouds, Wolfgangsee and Wallersee—see the water's surface shining?" We do. This *sight* plus the "*Sound* of Music" makes Austria irresistible.

By 8:55AM, we're floating northeastwards at 17 kmh and have reached our maximum altitude of 2,540m. Far from chilly, the heat from the gas jets makes me feel I'm in an outdoor sauna in the sky! Werner, all relaxed now, rotates the balloon so that we can all see its shadow, surrounded by a faint golden halo, on the clouds below. Then, all of a sudden, he hoists himself onto the edge of the basket, standing there over nothingness, to make some photographs of us—doubtless with our faces frozen in horror at the idea that he might fall off! Of course, he doesn't …

Finally, it's time to descend. All the while, Werner's been in walkie-talkie contact with Dieter, our driver, giving him our coordinates so he can follow us in the Land Rover, on the ground but invisible beneath the 300m high cloud cover. "Fahre nach Henndorf, da in etwa werden wir landen ("Drive to Henndorf, that's about where we'll be landing")" says Werner as we come down through the clouds and spy the forest-green velvet of the meadows directly below us.

But landing's not so simple; in fact, it proves to be the most hair-raising adventure of all! First, coming within 30 metres of the ground, we are swept over a copse of oak trees and I'm absolutely *sure* we'll land in the treetops and be tipped out, all of us. We ascend again, blasting the gas jets to get us out of there.

Next we find ourselves poised directly above a large, modern farm house with its rooftop solar panels staring us straight in the eye. A woman comes out, waves and says "Grüß Gott"—"God greet you"—but, God or not, she looks quite dubious about our coming to rest on her roof.

Close call-collision with a barn!

Blast the gas jets again, energetically, and ascend, now drifting softly towards a beckoning meadow. Ahh, that looks invitingly safe ... except that, once again, when we are no more than five metres above ground, we find ourselves irresistibly drawn towards a nearby orchard, with a three story barn just behind it! This is it! Impossible not to glide right into it. "*Gas geben*—step on the gas!" I gasp to myself, eyes riveted on the ripe plums, then bright red apples, as we glide past, close enough to pluck one! We clear the barn's roof by centimetres, no more, I'm sure, afraid to look.

Now hovering nervously above electricity lines for what seems like an eternity—what if we run out of gas??!! Werner, reading our minds it seems, says, "Not to worry. We always have gas reserves of at least 30% in each of the three tanks ... well, this one's down to 15% now, but we keep the reserves because landing a balloon is not so simple ... as you can see."

Meanwhile, we also see Dieter's Land Rover and trailer, followed by the convoy of family members' cars just turning into the road that will lead them to us. Now that's masterly coordination for you. As for us, we need a full fifteen minutes of manoeuvring before we finally manage to set down just at 10:00AM, right on the side of the small country road next to a farmhouse. "Well, that's about it," Werner says, wiping his brow, "1:32 hrs of flight and 13.2 km ... but don't anyone jump out of the basket yet, otherwise we'll take off again!"

The Land Rover has been tracking us and now pulls up right in front of us. Werner tells the guys to get out one at a time, then does a little bit of magic manipulation with the gas jets and muscle power so that the basket is perfectly positioned onto the trailer. Something tells me they've done this before!!

Then the balloon envelope is brought softly down onto the still dewy fields of clover, straightened, coiled and packed into the balloon bag, after which we get to sit on it, dew and all, to squeeze the extra air out. Then it's packed onto the trailer and off we go for the finale—our traditional "baptism by fire."

Soon sitting outdoors in the garden of the Irlingerhof overlooking the Mondsee, we order drinks while Werner prepares the "ceremony"— all eight of us have just survived and thrived on our first ballooning adventure. Each one is called by name to come before Werner and Dieter, kneel, be baptised by the fire (singeing our hair!) and blessed by the water (dousing the singe!), then raised to the peerage of the balloners' aristocracy and given a certificate to prove it. While a beaming 80-year-old Anna is enshrined as "Kaiserin" or "Empress," I receive the august title of *Comtesse Adrea, die mutige Wolken-schieberin zu Zell am Moos*"—that is, "Countess Adrea, the Courageous Cloud-Pusher of Zell am Moos." "Don't forget your title," Werner warns, "balloners take this seriously so it'll cost you a round if you do."

All good things must come to a close so, after exchanging email addresses and best wishes, the other passengers go their separate ways while Dieter and Werner give me a lift back to my hotel. On the way, of course, talk turns to "What next?"

"Well, there's always the Alpenüberquerung—the Trans-Alpine Balloon Express," Dieter says. "That's feasible only in winter, usually January or February. Depending on the wind and weather conditions, it takes three to four hours at speeds of up to 130 kmh in a basket open to the elements and an altitude of up to 6,000m—*with* oxygen, of course," he adds reassuringly. "We usually land somewhere near Venice and stay the night to celebrate."

Now wouldn't that be the perfect way to usher in a New Year? By the time they drop me off, I'm already on their waiting list. Nothing like instant addiction to make one decisive!

****

Back to earth and with our feet on the ground, Werner and Dieter drop me off in St. Gilgen for the next part of this multi-phase adventure.

Exquisitely imbedded like a Baroque jewel at the top of the hourglass-shaped Wolfgangsee, St Gilgen is best known today for its Mozart connections: his mother was born here and his sister Nannerl, a musical prodigy in her own right, lived here near the lake shore. The town is alive with colourful flowers, quaint shops and a waterfront teeming with people this time of the year.

Just as I arrive, the bells of the Pfarrkirche (parish church) are tolling noon and my tummy's 'tolling' hunger, reminding me that I haven't even had breakfast yet—too excited this morning—and already it's time for lunch! I stroll down through the park to the lakeside Fischer Restaurant right next to the boat dock.

Being in the province of Salzburg and having just had one heady "hot air" experience, I know exactly what I'll order as soon as I spy it on the menu: *Salzburger Nockerln*—a French-style soufflé that made its debut in the 16th century and a "hot air" dish so delicate—and notoriously difficult to keep from 'falling'—that it's considered the 'prima donna' of all Austrian desserts. Today it's my lunch.

Salzburger Nockerln with Cassis Sauce

Ingredients: Soufflé

1 ½ oz butter	*4 oz (1/2 cup) cream*	*½ tsp vanilla extract*
4 egg yolks	*3 oz sugar*	*2 T white wine*
1 ½ oz flour	*pinch of salt*	*8 egg whites*
	2T powdered sugar, sifted	*... and a silent prayer!*

Cassis Sauce:

5 T black currant jelly	*4 oz (1/2 cup) red wine*	*1 T honey*
1 tsp sugar, mixed with ...	*¼ tsp vanilla extract*	

Preheat the oven to 400-425 degrees F. Note: It is very important to preheat the oven to ensure that this very fragile soufflé bakes quickly. Whatever you do, don't open the oven door while the soufflé is baking or it might 'fall'—that is, collapse!

Combine butter, cream, vanilla extract and sugar in a pot and bring to a boil, beating constantly with a wire whisk. Remove from heat. Beat egg yolks and sugar until fluffy. Add white wine, sifted flour and salt and continue to beat until the batter is very creamy.

In a separate bowl, beat egg whites until very stiff (if necessary, add several drops of lemon juice). Fold quickly into egg yolk mixture. Butter and dust with powdered sugar a large, straight-sided ovenproof baking dish. Gently transfer batter to form three mounds. Place in oven immediately and bake for 12-16 min. or until golden brown.

While the soufflé is baking, prepare the cassis sauce by heating the currant jelly, together with the red wine, honey and vanilla extract. Bring to a boil and stir vigorously.

Spoon the soufflé onto individual plates, dust generously with powdered sugar and drizzle with cassis sauce. **Guten Appetit!**

SUMMER IN THE SALZKAMMERGUT: PARADISE FOUND!

JULY: A Taste Of Imperial Romance: Bad Ischl

The Emperor's annual pilgrimage to Bad Ischl put this picturesque spa town on the map and also made it "one of the most brilliant centres of fashionable life in Europe" until his death in 1916.

Bad Ischl—an elite summer getaway whose scintillating atmosphere might be compared with the 1960s aura of America's "Kennedy Compound" at Hyannis Port on Massachusetts' Cape Cod—was a very special enclave where sports and, more importantly, prestige and power met and mingled every summer. And "every" summer meant over 70 of them under the Hapsburg's longest-reigning Emperor, Franz Josef, whose annual Ischler pilgrimage put this picturesque spa town on the map and also made it "one of the most brilliant centres of fashionable life in *fin de siècle* Europe".

At only 18 years of age, Franz Josef had assumed the throne in very troubled times: Vienna's March Revolution of 1848 had just toppled Austria's long powerful Prince Metternich and Hungary was also staging an uprising that was finally suppressed only with the help of Russia. Thrown right into the thick of things, he was overnight transformed, outwardly at least, from a handsome young sovereign into the "workaholic" Emperor he remained for the next 68 years.

An extremely conscientious monarch, he lived a largely ascetic life in Vienna, regularly rising at 0400 each morning and often fighting his "Papierkreig" (paper war) until late into the night. Even though spontaneity had been ruthlessly drilled out of him, Franz Josef looked forward with longing to his summer escapes from Vienna's stifling officialdom. His *joie de vivre* was refreshed by the great outdoors of Austria's gorgeous Salzkammergut, strewn as it was with over 40 mountain-encircled lakes, and by contact with his rural subjects who lived simply and close to nature.

Of course, the paperwork followed Franz Josef and so did the people so that, over the course of decades, Bad Ischl hosted many of the crowned heads of Europe, besides acting as a magnet for the aristocracy and for artists of all persuasions (e.g. painters Ferdinand Waldmüller and Rudolf von Alt, writer Johann Nestroy and composers Anton Bruckner, Johann Strauss and Franz Lehár). Everyone who was anyone summered in Bad Ischl ... and the reason was Franz Josef.

Let's go back in time to one particular summer in Bad Ischl—the summer of 1853. The dashing young Emperor, by far Europe's most eligible bachelor, was again in residence, preparing to celebrate his 23rd birthday that fell on August 18th. His strong-willed mother, Archduchess Sophie, known as "the only man at the Court", was also preparing something: a special birthday surprise in the form of a future Empress to grace the Imperial Court and bed to produce more male Hapsburg heirs.

Thus it was that Sophie summoned her sister, Duchess Ludovika, to bring her eldest daughter, Hélène ('Nene'), from next door Bavaria to Ischl that summer to seal a nuptial agreement. Younger sister Sisi tagged along, her mother thinking that perhaps she'd catch the eye of the Emperor's younger brother Maximilian—yet another duet of politically induced marriages must have been on sisters' Sophie and Ludovika's mind ...

As for Franz Josef, despite the burden of the imperial crown, he was, after all, not unlike all young men who appreciated a pretty face and figure and perhaps, underneath the stiff court etiquette, yearned to meet someone who could give expression to this mostly repressed side of his life—the free-spirited spontaneity, the poetry and the passion.

Enter Elisabeth von Wittelsbach—fondly called "Sisi"—his 15-year-old first cousin, the Duchess of Bavaria, who had grown up living his passion for nature and who shared a common (and perhaps too close) genetic background. Enter Elisabeth and the stage was set for a taste of imperial romance ...

Elisabeth. Born on Christmas Eve 1837 with a "lucky tooth," the high-spirited young girl who later became 'the lonely Empress' was once-upon-her-childhood a rollicking tomboy, climbing trees and riding horses, swimming and fishing with her seven siblings at her parents' summer palace of Possenhofen on Bavaria's Starnbergsee. The third of eight children born to Duke Maximilian and Duchess Ludovika of Bavaria, she grew up mostly in the great outdoors, worlds away from the stiff etiquette of the Imperial Court. Despite familial problems—her mother suffered from depression and her father from insatiable appetites for everything from women to drink—Sisi grew up relatively care-free and unconcerned about her future ...

... until that fateful visit to Bad Ischl that changed her fifteen-year-old life forever.

Duchess Ludovika had presented her eldest daughter Hélène and the audience at the Villa Eltz was in full swing when Franz Josef caught sight of Elisabeth and—it was the proverbial "love as first sight"! Never mind Nene, Franz Josef proposed to Elisabeth instead! They announced their engagement the very next day—on the Emperor's birthday—and were married within the year. Thus began one of Europe's most beguiling but tragic romances that ended 44 years later when "Sisi" was assassinated in 1898 on the shores of Lake Geneva. But wait, let's not get ahead of ourselves.

Back in Bad Ischl, the euphoria of young love burned bright. Sisi was equally enthralled with Franz Josef, her only regret being that he was so famous—"if only he were a tailor," she is said to have confided to her adolescent dairy. Yet she could not escape this "call of destiny" and, with it, the necessity of leaving her carefree days behind her to enter onto the world's stage through marriage. She did so with the full fervor and candor of her personality, as revealed in a touching later poem that sought to recapture the effervescence of those initial days and months before the Court caught up with her:

> *I need not tell thee of the time*
> *Which once united us as intimate*
> *And which neither you nor I could ever forget*
> *However endlessly distant it may seem yet.*

> *Do you remember that sweet trice*
> *Where I from will-less frame*
> *Did kiss the soul from thy lips*
> *That it might ever more be mine?*

Their nine-month engagement gave Sisi just enough time to turn sixteen before their wedding and—this being before the days of mass media—all of Austria was beside itself with excitement to see its future Empress in the flesh. Thus, in April of 1854, Sisi and Franz Josef's bridal party was transported down the Danube (an updated variation on the *Niebelungenlied*) on a four-day trip with frequent stops so that Elisabeth could be seen by her subjects-to-be. A shy adolescent unprepared for her future role, this was the first of a life full of ordeals where Sisi felt herself exposed in the presence of strangers.

In Vienna at last, the formal marriage ceremony was performed with all pomp and circumstance at the Augustinerkirche on April 24th—her choice to marry in white allegedly launching a tradition that endures to this day—and the couple thought to escape to the lovely Laxenburg castle south of Vienna ... but they had not reckoned with Sophie, Sisi's ever-present mother-in-law, nor with the ongoing affairs of state that accompanied them, effectively thwarting any attempts at a real "honeymoon." This set the scene for the rest of their lives: though Franz Josef had married for love, he also believed himself to have been appointed by "divine sanction"—that is, by God himself!—to be Emperor; thus, politics and public duties would always come before all else for him. This was a brutal shock to the young bride who felt that she had forfeited her freedom for life in a gilded cage.

"Oh, that on the broad avenues of vanity I had never strayed!" she wrote in a poem only two weeks after her marriage, *"I have awakened in a dungeon … awakened from a rapture ….in which I gambled away you—Freedom—away."* She was right. Even though they continued the annual "summer freshness" treks to Bad Ischl, residing at the Kaiser Villa with its extensive park, the Salzkammergut was not far enough away and, more and more, Sisi found herself taking ever longer solitary journeys.

Loss of personal freedom (with tragic consequences) is the price paid by many public figures, from celebrities such as Romy Schneider, the actress who later embodied Sisi in a wildly popular film series about the Empress's life, to the British Princess Diana who suffered a similar fate (see below). In the case of Sisi, the "child Empress" was clearly meant to be symbolically "seen but not heard" and to conform to protocol within a draconian Spanish tradition.

Childbearing was the first order of the day. Sisi complied, giving birth to three children (one of them, Crown Prince Rudolf) in four years, by the time she was 21. But, as she later noted with chagrin, although she was good enough to give birth, she was seen as not old enough to take care of her own children, each of whom was immediately taken away by her mother-in-law to be "properly" brought up. Thus, after losing this key struggle, she distanced herself both from her children and from her husband, who further saddened her by admitting to sexual dalliances elsewhere. And so, bit by bit, the carefree young girl became the estranged Empress.

A remarkably beautiful woman as she matured—tall, slim, athletic, with thick dark chestnut hair that reached to her feet when let down, and an unmistakably majestic demeanour—Empress Elisabeth was often the subject of court portraits in her early years.

Although today's Vienna is awash in images of the exquisite young Empress—predictably Franz Xaver Winterhalter's official portrait of her in a bespangled ivory organdy gown with golden stars woven into her plaited chestnut hair (a sadly commercialized image that appears on everything from postcards to pastry boxes)—Vienna is, in fact, the very place Sisi came to avoid like the plague.

Small wonder. The Vienna of the fading Hapsburg Imperial Court—that hothouse of hereditary aristocracy with its uniformed, moustached, dandified men and tight-corseted court ladies whose main pastime was gaining favour with the Emperor while gossiping about his wife with the paparazzi of their day—was anathema to Sisi. Its rigid protocol stifled the life out of her, made her physically ill and finally drove her away in search of a place where she could again be that freedom-loving "self" whose spontaneity and love of life had captured Franz Josef's heart in the first place.

A restless soul that felt itself "coming from another star", she undertook a travel odyssey that led her to Madeira, Corfu, Venice and, fatefully years later, her last one to the shores of Lake Geneva in a ceaseless search for home.

"Sisi": The "Princess Diana" of her Day?

The similarities are striking between the odysseys of these two public personas—Empress Elisabeth and Princess Diana—both of whom were legends during their own lifetimes.

They captivated people with their initial freshness and innocence, remarkable natural beauty and joie de vivre, their exuberant love of nature, sports and travel, their motherhood and their natural warmth in dealing with people they valued, and their growing charisma and nurturance of their own image. Each created an ineffable aura that persists to this day.

But behind these public personas, the striking similarities persisted in more disturbing ways, imposed in part by the "traditions" under which they lived.

Both Sisi and Diana were plucked, while only in their teens, from a carefree life in relative obscurity and skyrocketed to "stardom". Both of the men who sought their hands in marriage—a "divinely sanctioned" Emperor and a king-in-waiting to the British throne—were part of the establishment who, for all their momentary enchantment, were actually seeking consorts rather than partners, mothers for their children and, in less complimentary terms, "trophy wives."

Once betrothed and their lineage secured through the birth of an heir, they turned their attentions largely elsewhere, whether politics or polo, leaving their displaced wives to fend for themselves. And of course, while women were to enter marriage as virgins, their husbands suffered no such stricture. Thus, both Sisi and Diana were betrayed sexually and misunderstood psychologically. Is it any wonder that they felt deceived and disrespected, exploited by a royalty that, at its worst, reduced women to breed mares and a court protocol that critiqued their every move? As a result, both Sisi and Diana developed eating disorders in an attempt to cope and both eventually went to great lengths to withdraw from the fray, only to have it catch up with them in the form of brutal deaths.

Whether Sisi could have ever become "the people's princess" as Diana did is an open question. In fact, they both began their odysseys much adored, but Sisi had neither instant media coverage nor acceptable opportunities beyond the Court for such personal contacts or humanitarian work although she did display her love of Hungary and was crowned Queen in 1867.

Nevertheless, Sisi and Diana were two women who, despite all the public scrutiny and private pain, have remained enduringly fascinating, enigmatic and, in the end, tragically symbolic figures of a society in which even the most elevated of women often remain victims of "tradition."

History notes with some chagrin that, despite it auspicious beginnings, the marriage of Sisi with Franz Josef proved a failure. She appeared to have lived intimately with him for only the first four years of their 44-year-long marriage and, in later life, actually took it upon herself to pair her husband up with the actress Katharina Schratt. Twenty-three years his junior, the actress became the Emperor's "lady friend" for the last 30 years of his life. They spent a good deal of time together in the Schratt Villa in Bad Ischl, which is now a public museum.

All the while, the Imperial Court and the upper crust of Austrian society continued to escape for "Sommerfrische"—summer freshness—in the region's unspoiled mountains and lakes. Villas and hunting lodges sprang up and, along with them, spa hotels, operetta concert halls and "Konditoreien" or pastry shops, the best-known among them being k.u.k. Zauner, established in 1832. One of its specialties was one of Kaiser Franz Josef's, too, named "Kaiserschmarrn" in his honour.

Kaiserschmarrn—The Emperor's Pancakes

Legend has it that the K&K court chef actually created the dish for Empress Elizabeth, wife of Austrian Emperor Franz Josef I, calling it 'Kaiserinschmarrn', but since the famously slim and athletic Empress wouldn't go touch anything with so many calories (at least not in public!), the dish was re-dedicated to the Emperor who was known for his sweet tooth!

Ingredients:

2 oz raisins	2-3 T rum
5 oz flour	pinch of salt
1 T powdered sugar, sifted	½ tsp vanilla extract
Grated rind ½ lemon	1 tsp lemon juice
3 egg yolks, light beaten	3 egg whites
4 oz (1/2 cup) milk	ground almonds (optional)
2-3 oz butter or margarine	2 T powdered sugar, sifted (decoration)

… and a bit of the Emperor's sweet tooth!

Stew the raisins, drain and drizzle them with rum. Sift flour into a large bowl. Beat in salt, powdered sugar, vanilla, grated lemon rind, egg yolks and milk until smooth. Let stand 20-30 min.

Now beat the egg whites with powdered sugar and a few drops of lemon juice until very stiff. If desired, add ground almonds. Fold whites into batter.

Melt butter in a large skillet. Our in batter, sprinkle with raisins. Cover. Heat until underside is golden brown. Turn. Using two forks, gently pull pancake into bite-sized pieces and complete cooking, stirring and turning pieces often. Serve hot, sprinkled generously with powdered sugar.

For pizzazz! Serve Kaiserschmarrn with cranberries, apple sauce or stewed fruits (e.g. plums). This can be either a main dish—it was one of Kaiser Franz Joseph's favourites!—or, in smaller portions, as a scrumptious dessert. ***Guten appetit!***

Cycling the Salzkammergut: "Salzkammergutradweg": This 345 km cycling route through the Salzkammergut is part of the „slow travel" theme of this book. Rather than rushing past on the Westautobahn with just glimpses of the Attersee and Mondsee, we're going to cruise around 13 lakes—notably the Attersee, Mondsee, Fuschlsee and Traunsee plus many smaller, less well-known ones—included on this route „under our own steam". And we'll *need* some "steam" to manage the total altitude difference of 1,850m!

We begin in Gmunden on the Traunsee with a boat trip that takes us and our bikes past the sheer rock face of the Traunstein. We get off at the far end of the lake and cycle to Bad Ischl for a leisurely lunch, then continue on late in the afternoon to Strobl on the Wolfgangsee where we spend a second night.

Next morning, still blessed by the weather, we cycle up the south-western side of the Wolfgangsee, taking a swimming break on the way, for lunch in St. Gilgen. After taking a stroll along the lakefront, we pedal on up over the pass that brings us to the Mondsee where we cycle the southwest side of the lake again until we reach the town of Mondsee where we overnight in a small bed and breakfast. In the evening, we take an hour-long evening boat tour around the lake.

The fourth overnight finds us back on the Attersee, after a long day of cycling from Mondsee up and all round the Zellersee, down the northeast side of the Mondsee and over to Unterach. Our last day holds a special treat: today's one of the few days in the year when cars are actually banned to give cyclers the right of way. Underway before

0800, we savour the cool morning, appreciate the good signage and quality of the road surfaces, and make a full round of this, the largest lake in the area.

For full information, please contact:

Oberösterreich Tourismus Information
Tel.: +43(0)732/22 10 22,

info@oberoesterreich.at,

http://www.oberoesterreich.at

SALZBURGERLAND TOURISMUS
Tel.: +43(0)662/6688-44

info@salzburgerland.com

http://www.salzburgerland.com

PRECIOUS SALT: HALLSTATT TO GOSAUSEE

Hallstatt. What a remarkable place! Dubbed by German world explorer and naturalist Alexander von Humboldt as "the world's most beautiful lakeside village", Hallstatt lives up to its epithets. Perched on steep rocky slopes within hearing distance of the thundering Mühlbach waterfall that plunges right through the village, Hallstatt's houses are built in crowded tiers that teeter precariously over the shining silver mirror of the fjord-like Hallstättersee.

We've arrived by bike as part of our Salzkammergut Cycling Trail, using a tunnel blasted through solid rock in 1966 to arrive at the town's portal. But, for centuries, the only way to get here was either on foot or by boat. Even later trains could only be accommodated on the far shore of the lake so that most travellers got their first view of Hallstatt from the boat that met the train and brought them across.

Not only is Hallstatt strikingly beautiful, it is also the site of the prehistoric Iron Age civilization named after it (Hallstatt Era 800-400 BC) when the villages were built on stilts along the steep fjord-like shores of its immeasurably deep lake. Hallstatt later became a key salt-mining center in the Hapsburg Empire's Salzkammergut. Today visiting these salt mines has been made more tourist-friendly.

PRECIOUS SALT—ONCE WORTH ITS WEIGHT IN GOLD!

When we think of the most vital trading commodities throughout history, gold, diamonds, silk and even oil rush to mind. And yet the former value of salt—today's inexpensive white granules—is often forgotten.

Once upon a time literally worth its weight in gold, salt has played a vital role in nearly every civilization since the beginning of time. In general use long before recorded history, salt was used to preserve and improve the taste of food, as money and as a spiritual icon. Below a few examples:

- *The first recorded reference to salt dates back almost 5,000 years when the Chinese described 40 different kinds of salt in a pharmacological book written in 2700 BC;*

- *Salt was first mentioned in a religious context in the Book of Job, written around 2250 BC;*

- *Pre-civilization "salt men" are a significant archaeological research source and Austria's Salzkammergut gave its name to an entire period (Hallstatt Era, 800-400 BC);*

- *Ancient Egyptians used salt to preserve food—and mummies—while Ethiopians used salt disks as a form of currency;*

- *The far-flung trade in ancient Greece involving the exchange of salt for slaves gave rise to the expression of someone being "not worth his salt";*

- *The Romans paid their soldiers partly in salt, this custom evolving into the word "salary";*

- *The French Revolution was sparked, in part, by a salt tax and later many of Napoleon's troops died during their retreat from Moscow due to a lack of salt;*

- *In the United States, the Erie Canal was built largely to transport salt; and*

- *In Slavic countries to this day, the salt given to brides and grooms symbolizes health and happiness.*

Of course, all salt deposits began as salty water; brine from seas, oceans and salt lakes. Even today's landlocked countries like Austria got their underground salt deposits from the evaporation of sea water, eons ago. Along the Mediterranean coast at the beginning of Roman times, the sea level was several meters below present levels and salt extraction was widely practiced. Then these salt flats were gradually inundated until about 400 AD. Rome's port had to be shifted inland three times. The overall effect of this sea level rise to nearly 2 m above present day levels was devastating for western European salt makers. During the 'Dark Ages' salt traffic almost disappeared and many inundated coastlines became deserted. Then, from about 700 AD, the sea level began receding again, coastal flats re-emerged and the fight over salt began anew.

Early trade routes and many of the first roads were established for transporting salt and many early civilizations levied taxes on it. As in Austria, the customs and salt tax 'limes' delineating the local inland salt monopoly became the future frontier lines of today's 'sovereign' states or provinces. By the fifteenth century, salt was obtained by boiling brine from salt springs, and many towns and cities in Europe were located near such sources, with names like "Salzburg", Hall-" and "Bad" linking their existence to nearby salt deposits. Thus, Austria's Salzkammergut was literally the Crown Salt Lands, a holding of utmost economic importance to the Hapsburg Empire long before it became treasured for its scenic beauty.

So now we know. Salzburg, the capital of the Salzkammergut or "Crown Salt Lands", means "salt citadel" in German, and the names of its villages—Bad Ischl, Hallein and Hallstatt— attest to the salt wealth of this region. Hallstatt, about 32 miles southeast of Salzburg and declared a UNESCO World Heritage Site in 1998, is undoubtedly one of the most picturesque.

Exploring Hallstatt's Hidden Treasures. Hallstatt still has the feel of a few centuries ago—no cars, no noisy malls, not even a real supermarket to speak of—instead, a Brigadoon-like village of clustered houses and church steeples clinging to the steep slopes that plunge straight into the unmeasured depths of the fjord-like Hallstättersee. No matter what weather, it exudes it other-worldly *atmosphere* at all seasons of the year.

Today we're in luck though. It's dazzlingly clear as John and I park our bikes where the cars are kept and saunter through the sun-drenched town, taking in its quaint wooden, multi-storey houses with their window boxes overflowing with geraniums and the small shops displaying local ceramics and woodcarvings.

Then we head for the funicular that will take us up to one of Hallstatt's biggest attractions—its salt mines that were a main source of wealth, livelihood—and death—in centuries past, as the terraced ossuary next to the village's churchyard attests.

As the cog railway whisks us up, the town recedes beneath us, replaced by a panoramic view of the glaciered Dachstein Massive. We alight to find ourselves in an alpine meadow full of wildflowers—yellow buttercups, electric blue gentian, pink primrose and lavender alpine soldanella—scattered richly about the rain-green meadows.

We walk up a gentle grade and soon arrive at the entrance to the old mine offices that now caters to tourists instead of miners. We pay and are sent to don special protective gear over our own light summer biking clothes: bulky cotton jackets and draw-string trousers with a leather insert in the seat of the pants—we'll soon see why! John gets a kick out of our unisex look!

Thus attired, we exit and ascend a steep path that bring us to the start of our visit in front of two huge, vault-like wooden doors cut into the forbidding face of the mountain. Here we are met by a young man (probably a summer-jobbing Austrian student) who gives us the basic history plus practical details in three languages: German, English and Italian.

Just as he wraps up his spiel, reminding us that it will be chilly, damp and dark inside and that we should stay together (as if anyone would want to stray far in an underground salt mine!), a small train appears on a equally small-gauge track. The driver sits astride the engine that pulls what resembles several toy train cars made out of large logs, halved lengthwise. The guide tells us to climb aboard and keep our arms and legs close in on the coming ride.

Clambering aboard along with another 40-odd brave souls, we straddle the logs and hold onto the person in front of us. The conductor toots his horn and off we go—right into the maw of the mountain—that opens its creaky doors at our approach. A chilly draught of damp air rushes out to accost us as the door clanks shut behind. We are rolling along, encased in all but total darkness, some kids behind us squealing with a mixture of fright and delight.

Some Austrians boys are also macho-yodelling but I'm too preoccupied with the narrowness of this tunnel all around us to feel festive. When the occasional overhead light pops up, it reveals us to be in the body of a giant earthworm that is crawling through solid rock as though it were nothing! The walls are fingertip close to us—keep your hands and feet in, the guide had said, with good reason! That's my excuse to hug John, sitting just in front of me.

After a short time, the train stops at a wide spot in the tunnel. This will be our initiation into subterranean tobogganing! We've arrived at a wooden slide that descends about ten meters and was once used by miners to arrive quickly at their worksite. The slide comprises two smooth wooden rails; we sit down in between them, our legs dangling over the side.

We watch the others, singing their respective "odes to joy" as they rocket downward, and then it's our turn. John and I sit in tandem, me embracing him, atop the slide. We push off, lean way back as they've told us and zoom deeper down into the "bowels of the earth". Whizzing down this slide turns me into a kid again and I let out a whoop as well just as the slide begins to flatten out after five seconds or so. We dismount and find ourselves in a sort of underground amphitheatre where we watch a short film on the history of salt mining and its technical evolution through the centuries—how it brought the riches today associated with oil to these outlying areas.

Now we continue our underground trek, following our guide, single file, through a labyrinth of dark, damp passages blasted out of the rock.

It's hard to know whether we're going up or down, much less in which direction. But when I touch the damp wall and then put my fingertip to my tongue, guess what? It's really salty!

After about seven minutes, we arrive at a second slide, longer and steeper than the first. Deeper still into the maw of the mountain. We slide again and, this time, the seat of my pants really starts to heat up! Just as I'm on the verge of spontaneous combustion, the slide flattens out and I'm spared a devil's martyrdom.

Our guide leads us to the shore of a large underground lake formed by the salt extraction process. Hypnotically still and totally transparent, the water's surface perfectly mirrors the cavern's ceiling of stalactites. But it's a salty mirror and when our guide tosses in a small stone, the "mirror" shatters like a fine crystal goblet dropped on a marble floor. No ripples.

We explorers keep walking, single file, Indian-style, through endless tunnels until—all at once!—two medieval mine workers appear! Seemingly illuminated by the torches they hold aloft, their faces are creased with fatigue and their backs bent under the bags of salt they carry … but their eyes stare unseeing. It's a very life-like diorama carved into a rock recess.

Catching our breath and calming down, finally we come to a tight spiral staircase that we climb to a small wooden room, then one last seemingly endless 400m tunnel, after which we stand there, huddling in the dark for what seems like an eternity. John is holding my hand and the boys have long since stopped their yodelling by the time we spy a tiny light that grows larger as it approaches with that unmistakable clakety-clack sound.

Our train has come to fetch us! Longing for light, we squeeze aboard for our long last ride to freedom. Again, two vault-like doors swing open and there we are! Only the sun has fled during our two hours underground. We quickly change and sprint for the funicular that takes us down. But now it all looks transformed. It's only mid-afternoon but already the sky is a glowering purple, the mountains are cloaked in silver clouds and wisps of vapour linger over the lake and hover ethereally over

Hallstatt's roofs and steeples. The village has taken on the dreamlike unreality of a mist-shrouded Japanese scroll.

After our subterranean adventure, we decide to stay the night in this tiny, picturesque village. We have something to look forward to since Hallstatt is also the site of one of Austria's best known wood-carving school, not to mention a macabre collection of skulls and bones from previous centuries exhibited right next to the Protestant cemetery. Burial space being a scarce commodity on these very steep lakeshore slopes, the bodies had to be excavated at regular intervals and the bones stored "cheek by jowl," so to speak.

That trip through the salt mines has definitely whetted our appetite! We take the cable car back down and scamper into the closest Gasthof just as ping-pong-ball-sized hail stones begin to pelt down to enjoy a well-deserved late lunch.

Veal Birds (Kalbsvögerl)

Song birds, especially larks, were fair game in many parts of Austria where "bird catching" remained a profession well into the 19ᵗʰ century. These delicious veal birds were sometimes tastier than the "real thing."

Ingredients:

4-6 slices of veal	*salt*	*2 oz bacon*
4 oz ground meat	*4 T cream*	*1 egg yolk, beaten*
1 medium onion, chopped	*pinch of thyme*	*1 garlic clove, crushed*
1 small onion, chopped	*3 oz bacon, diced*	*3 oz stewed vegetables*
	1 cup (8 oz) beef stock	

Sauce:

½ cup (4 oz) sour cream	*1-2 T flour*	*4 oz cooked mushrooms*

Trim the edges of the ½ thick veal slices, rinse and dry. Pound the meat with a cleaver, rub with salt and pepper. Make the filling as follows: chop the bacon fine and sauté until golden brown. Combine with ground meat in a bowl. Add cream, ½ of the chopped onions, egg yolk, steamed vegetables, thyme and crushed garlic. Spread a thin layer of filling on each slice of meat. Roll the meat, secure with skewers or thread.

Dredge the birds in flour. Sauté the remaining onions with diced bacon. Then sauté the birds in the onion/bacon mixture until golden brown. Add stock and reduce heat. Cover and simmer for 40-50 min. until tender.

Remove the birds and take out the skewers or thread. To make pan gravy: Add flour to the sour cream and stir until smooth. Add this to the pan juices and bring o a boil. Add mushrooms. Season to taste. Immerse the birds in the gravy for several minutes and serve immediately. **Guten appetit!**

GETTING THERE

By train: Rail Europe (08708 371371; www.raileurope.co.uk) can sell you a ticket from London Waterloo to Salzburg via Brussels or Paris.

By plane: The nearest airport is Salzburg, which is served by Austrian Airlines. To reduce the impact on the environment, you can buy an "offset" from Climate Care (01865 207 000; www.climatecare.org). The environmental cost of a return London-Salzburg flight is £1.70 (used to fund sustainable energy projects).

STAYING THERE. Hallstatt has 12 small family-run hotels, such as the Gasthof Pension Hallberg (The Divers Inn) at Seestrasse 113 (00 43 6134 8709; www.pension-hallberg.at.tf). Doubles start at €70 (£50), including breakfast.

VISITING THERE. Hallstatt and Altausee Salt Mine (00 43 6132 200 2400; www.salzwelten.at).

FURTHER INFORMATION. Hallstatt tourist information: 00 43 6134 8208; www.hallstatt.net and the Austrian Tourist Board: 0845 101 1818; www.austria.info/uk

SUMMER IN THE SALZKAMMERGUT: PARADISE FOUND!

AUGUST: Heaven's Gate And St Wolfgang's Pilgrimage

The *Schafbergbahn* is the name of the cogwheel train, inaugurated by Emperor Franz Josef himself in the year 1893, that will take me to the top of the mountain called the "Rigi of the Eastern Alps" for its incomparable 360° alpine vistas.

The original train, one of the first in Europe, had a coal-burning engine and a small-gauge track enhanced by an innovative cogwheel arrangement that helped the engine, as well as the brakes, on this sometimes quite steep route.

Today's version is more modern but still chugs off—celebrated by bells and whistles, jolts and bumps—on its 40-minute panorama ride to the top. As we as ascend, the lake emerges from between the trees and it feels almost like being in a glider floating upwards, above it all. As I plan to stay the night on the top, I arrive with the last train and see two others, packed full with day guests, heading down.

The Berghotel Schafbergspitze—the mountain hotel at the summit of the 1,783m Schafberg, or "sheep mountain"—was built in 1860 in response to growing interest in alpine tourism and has now been in the hands of the Pasch family for several generations. Cordially greeted by father and son, they point out some lakes we ballooned over a few weeks ago, now seen from a different perspective: the Wolfgangsee, Mondsee, Fuschlsee, Attersee, Irrsee, Krottensee and Chiemsee, the latter in Bavaria. They also name the summits that fill the entire skyline from left to right: Dachstein Massiv, Bishop's Mitre, Hochkönig, Tennengebirge, Hoher Göll, Watzmann (latter two also in Bavaria) and the Gaisberg overlooking Salzburg.

After a half-hour walk along the ridge of the sheer north face that drops some 700m to the three small alpine lakes (Karseen) I'll be passing on tomorrow's hike, I return for a light supper and exquisitely serene sunset on the hotel's terrace. Then the sky darkens, clouds roll in and we are even treated to Nature's own fireworks—heat lightening (Wetterleuchten) that sizzles the night sky for more than an hour. I fall asleep thinking the tour for tomorrow will be a write-off.

Happily not. When I awaken just at sunrise, the sky is brilliantly clear, washed clean in the night, and I pack quickly, have breakfast, say goodbye to Family Pasch and embark on my day's discovery.

The Himmelspforte—Heaven's Gate—is just that: it opens into outer space! The vertical North Face of the mountain. This tour starts at the high point, both literally and figuratively, with a vertical descent aided by steel cables and rings to hold onto. Otherwise there's nothing but air plus the two Austrian Alpine Club signs at the entrance that read: "Rock falls around Heaven's Gate: proceed at your own risk!" and "Alpine Erfahrung, Trittsicherheit und Schwindelfreiheit erforderlich"—alpine experience, surefootedness and freedom from vertigo required". What have I gotten myself into?!

My knees are shaky, my stomach's queasy, I consider turning back … but then I take a deep yogic breath, get a grip on myself—and more importantly, a grip on the steel cable riveted into the rock—and start down. Alone. In fact, I love climbing in the mountains and have done hundreds of tours, mostly with my Austrian former husband who is an expert mountaineer and skier, and Renate, my Austrian 'Bergkamarad' for over a decade.

I find myself addicted to the NOW moment of mountaineering: everything concentrated, all my possessions and "proviant" pared down and packed into a single rucksack; all attention on the actions at hand (and foot). All of existence concentrated in each single moment, moving with care and precision as climbing (or descending) becomes a slow-motion ballet.

The first half-hour is the worst/best because I'm out of the routine (and out of condition). The more I inch my way down, the more the sheer rock face rises up above me. Grateful for my telescoping ski/ hiking poles, I descend the tiny zig-zag path along a steep shoulder strewn with rocks that have fallen from—guess where? Keep moving, I tell myself, reciting "144, 144"—Austria's emergency rescue telephone number is my mantra for this morning—praying that my cell phone's still charged.

But it gets better, the farther I descend and, little by little, I get into the swing of things. Now I'm really glad to be here. Fabulous views enhanced by being alone in the total early morning stillness. Traversing now under the entire length of the Schafberg's north face, its silver flank rearing up like a Lipizzaner in stone, I'm euphoric. Two young Austrians meet me now on their way up but otherwise, I've got this paradise all to myself. Incredible!

After 1.5 hours I arrived at the "malerische Mittersee"—picturesque Mittersee—and, still solitary, dangle my feet in the water while enjoying a little snack. Dragonflies, neon blue-and-green, dart about and check me out. Back underway, I climb up and cross a ridge before coming to the next lake, the Mönichsee. Here it's almost crowded: four Austrians, four cows, four sheep, and me! I dip my feet gingerly into the water and … it's warm! In I go for a refreshing swim before the final descent. One more hour and I've arrived back at the Schafbergbahn station on the lakefront.

Once again—and no wonder after that hike!—hunger calls just as the passenger boat arrives at the dock and I decide to hop on and be delivered to my very favorite spot in the whole Salzkammergut: the Gasthof zum Lachsen, a "secret hideaway" discovered back in 1971 that was the setting for my decision to make Austria my home over thirty years ago.

Disembarking at the Falkensteiner dock seven minutes later, I stroll the 100 remaining metres along a narrow, enchanting lakefront road dotted mostly with private villas amidst meadows of wildflowers. Tucked away here near the end of this road that is blocked from continuing around the lake by an enormous rock outcropping lies "my" Gasthof, a small two-story country inn with accommodations. White stucco below, its upper façade is rich, old, dark-timbered set off by crimson geranium-overflowing flower boxes. Its spacious, deep green, tree-shaded lawn descends gently to a slender dock that juts far out into the blue-green lake. Entering this sanctuary under its arch of chestnut trees, I spy the Gasthof's two tame swans as they parade towards the lake, wagging their tails behind them. On the water, another of the 19th century passenger paddleboats crosses behind a classic wooden piroge with its patient fisherman. It's a time warp bringing together two different epochs.

Things just don't change that quickly around here; that's part of their charm. In fact, the inn itself scarcely looks different than it must have shortly after it was built in the year 1600 by local fishermen and farmers, its location linked to the fabled hermit monk St Wolfgang, who lived on the Falkenstein outcropping in the 10th century. When this secluded site later became an important pilgrimage, the inn started providing beer to thirsty pilgrims.

The year 1856 was the year of the "big fish" for it was then that a giant salmon—two metres long and 30-kg in weight—was caught here, thus giving the Gasthof zum Lachsen its name. Granted, the fish I order for lunch, a so-called "Reinanke" that has just been fished out of the drinking-quality water of the Wolfgangsee, won't be that huge. Still, the baked filet is as big as a turkey breast. My waiter, son of the Falkensteiner family that has run this inn for over a century, tells me that while the other well-known local catch, the "Saibling" is a "noble" relative of the trout, both those fish are hunters, whereas the Reinanke is a vegetarian fish that lives off plankton. To go with it, I have Gemüse Gröstl (roasted vegetables) that includes zucchini, summer squash, Brussels sprouts, cabbage and thin potato slices.

Sitting in the Indian Summer sunshine at the top of the lawn, my healthy and delicious lunch is accompanied by a Schloß Gobelsburg Riesling Urgestein from Langenlois in Austria's Kamptal.

Gebackene Reinanke Filet mit Gemüse Gröstl

Ingredients:

1 large Reinanke trout, filleted	*Olive oil for baking*
2 eggs, parsley, lemon wedges	*Salt, flour, bread crumbs*

Salt the trout filet, let it stand for 10 minutes, then dry it off. Dip both sides of the filet first in flour, then in the lightly salted raw egg, and finally in bread crumbs. Then lower into hot oil and let it fry to a golden brown hue. Remove and place on a bed of vegetable Gröstl, decorated with parsley and lemon wedges.

Gröstl Ingredients:

2 zucchini, 2 summer squash,   *6-8 Brussels sprouts,*

¼ head white cabbage   *2 small potatoes*

Roast the vegetables quickly at high heat to retain their colour and crisp texture. Add a dash of the fish sauce and serve steaming hot.

Wine: *Schloß Gobelsburg Riesling Urgestein from Langenlois in Austria's Kamptal.*

Guten Apetit!

"Gestärkt"—German for "fortified"—I'm ready for my next beckoning adventure: a delicious and well-deserved, night's sleep!

From Attersee to St. Wolfgang: Himmelfahrt and Fireworks

Although today's Austria is increasingly international, to truly appreciate its history and culture, you have to understand the riches of its religious traditions. Catholicism was long the official religion and is still actively practiced by the vast majority of Austrians, especially those in the countryside. Also, the cultural patronage of the Church through the ages has been the source of many of the country's great achievements in the arts, architecture and music. The following vignette is a blend of religious and cultural traditions, with some spectacular scenery thrown in for good measure.

Celebrating Catholicism and wine cultures

Today, August 15th, is a special day: Maria Himmelfahrt or Maria's Ascension Day. It's 0600 and I'm up to have some time to myself before attending a festive choral mass in the *Marien-Wallfahrtskirche*—Maria's pilgrimage church—in the village of Attersee located on the lake of the same name, the largest in the Salzkammergut and the largest lake fully within Austria's boundaries (the larger Lake Constance shares borders with Germany and Switzerland while the eastern Neusiedlersee shares its borders with Hungary).

I'm going to mass with Melanie, a longtime Austrian friend whose two daughters went to the Vienna International School and the Scouts together with my own daughter over 20 years ago. Though my UN work took me away from Austria for 16 years, Melanie and I kept up our friendship, as well as the faith that binds us and the Austrian way of life together.

Austria, for us, means a deep sense of community, also spiritual community. And it is Melanie who introduced me to Pater Josef who welcomed me into his Cursillo community in Vienna when I returned to Austria in 2002. I had wanted to acknowledge this by doing a pilgrimage and asked Pater Josef, who is Spanish by birth, about Santiago de Compostela. But he revealed that there's another one, much closer at hand, that has been here all along. It's the St Wolfgang pilgrimage over the Falkenstein—one that I've even walked several times, though apparently in the wrong direction. So today I'll do it right.

But first for the mass. This one, celebrating Maria's ascension to Heaven, is held in the slender-spired Maria pilgrimage church where I'm to meet Melanie at 0900, but by the time I leave the house, the heavens have decided to show their bounteous nature by pouring out rain by the bucketful. It keeps up as I make my way through the maze of church festival—or "Kirtag"—stands set up for this day. By the time I finally get inside and meet Melanie, we're both soggy as sponges.

But that's quickly forgotten in the splendor of the place—all immaculate white-and-gold inside and full of candles and the smell of incense from the 0800 mass preceding ours. The "pillars of the community," mostly families with children, smiling and greeting one another with the traditional "Grüß Gott"—God greet you!—have just spilled out of the church dressed in their festive traditional dress, or "trachten" finery. The mood is set before we even enter.

Outside it's pelting down, which makes inside all the more cozy, rosy and festive. The church holds only about 200 people. An enormous Baroque altar occupies the entire front with its gold-leaf Maria and Child, surrounded by saints and lit by 12 tall candles and dozens of small votive ones on the altar. Above and behind us stands the organ and the 45-strong choir from the neighboring village of St. Georgen that comes to sing each year for this occasion.

The service is performed in German by an Austrian priest, assisted by a black priest from Ghana sent especially from his post at the Vatican. They are surrounded by a good dozen altar boys and girls in white robes and crimson cowls. Soon the choir chimes in, a golden braid of voices, soprano over alto, then bass over baritone, weaving sacred melodies. The service concludes with holy communion and an invitation to carry the joy of this ascension with us throughout our day, our lives.

After the service, Melanie and I stroll briefly through the *Kirtag* (church festival) stands offering everything from used books to clothing to kebabs, and then drive to the local Hotel Haberl for lunch. Overlooking the lake, it enjoys a reputation for good food and friendliness.

Feeling replenished and "rarin' to go", Melanie and I set off from the Attersee along the romantic lakefront road to Unterach and then across to the neighbouring Mondsee (Moon Lake), finally winding our way up a forested hill and over the top into St. Gilgen on the Wolfgangsee. Here we board the paddleboat steamer for the short ride over to Fürberg where our modern day "pilgrimage" begins.

In the footsteps of St. Wolfgang: The Falkenstein pilgrimage

Legend has it that Bishop Wolfgang lived in the 10th century in Regensburg (today's Germany) but fled the city in 976 because of a civil war. He came to the mountain called the Falkenstein (Falcon Rock) above this lake where he spent years as a recluse and allegedly had more than his share of encounters with the devil. At one point, he threw his axe from the mountain down to the shoreline below, vowing to build a church wherever it landed. That site is today the exquisite church of St Wolfgang with its renowned winged altar by Michael Pacher, one of Austria's most famous 17th century architects.

As many times as I've been here, I hadn't realized til yesterday that, after being a pagan worship site, in the late Middle Ages St Wolfgang became one of the most important pilgrimage sites in the Christian world, with alleged miracle cures from a spring. Melanie tells me that pilgrims came on foot from as far away as Cracow and Magdeburg, carrying heavy stones up the steep path to deposit them at the top as an act of repentance. As for me, I've only come from Geneva and that by train and am carrying only an extra stone or so in weight ... which I'd be only to happy to leave at the top.

With that in mind, we set out on our two hour trek from Fürberg over the Falkenstein to the picturesque village of Ried by St. Wolfgang ... in the rain! As if by divine decree, after seven weeks of sweltering heat with the driest weather and highest temperatures ever recorded in this part of the world (over 40ºC), today the rain pours down. But that doesn't deter us—or the fifty or so mountain bikers pedaling or pushing their way up one side and down the other of this quite steep and rocky path. A modern-day exercise in repentance? In any case, most of the way is in the woods and the cooling rain is welcome.

There are 24 stations on this Pilgrim's Way. After about half an hour of steep ascent, we come to the church in the Falkenstein where pilgrims were housed; then another 15 minutes or so to the "wondrous caves and wishing bells" and later the magic spring whose waters are said to cure eye diseases.

Coming down after the high point of this hike, we are delighted to see the meadows of Ried stretching out below, reaching right to the shores of the lake. Having spent many a visit here, once for an entire month, it's like coming home and we head for Haus Falkenstein to catch the boat back to St. Gilgen.

Fireworks over the Attersee

Back on the neighbouring Attersee and noting that the weather has improved, about eight of us pack ourselves into two cars, make our way to Unterach and stroll out to the lakefront for a delightful hour of prism-colored water fountains and sparkling fireworks to the tunes of festive marches, then waltzes and finally even a rousing French Can-Can.

By the time we get home it's almost midnight and tomorrow we have cycling on our agenda—but now I still have to write before calling the night a day, which, at 0104 in the morning, it technically is.

Next morning I'm up early to say farewell to Melanie before heading back to Vienna and my "day job".

AUTUMN (MOSTLY) IN THE MOUNTAINS. BERG HEIL! SEPTEMBER: "Der Berg Ruft!": Dachstein To Kaprun

From Traunsee to the Dachstein Glacier to the Ramsau

Let's stay on the Salzkammergut biking track since it's one of the many that can be done in stages. Now it's early autumn and I'm back, but this time with John, another long-time American friend and serious cycler/mountain biker, and Jean, my friend who's visiting from Geneva. We've driven out from Vienna with John's bike rack loaded and stayed the night in Gmunden on the Traunsee.

Up really early this September morn, we want to get in some quality biking time before the heat drives us to forsake our "saddles" for a cool swim in one of the tempting lakes. Now, it's absolutely still, so still I'm sure that if we stopped and went into the nearby fields, we could actually "hear the corn growing" (if it hadn't already been harvested!)

We cruise the empty country roads (Hwy 145 in this case), skirting Bad Ischl and on to Bad Goisern where we start our day's cycling. Jean's going to drive the car to meet us at the Gosausee.

When John and I set out, wisps of clouds still cling like sleep to the mountainsides but we're soon wide awake with exertion. From the ascending valley floor, the surrounding landscape becomes more vertical and fjordlike, the closer we get to Hallstatt where things turns spectacular, sheer walls plummeting into the bottomless lake that is the Hallstättersee.

Thank heavens it's not hot! Still, I'm fairly panting as we turn off towards now onto Route 166 that will take us up to Gosau. Entering the narrow cut of a thickly wooded glacial gorge, we follow the twisting two-lane road as it threads its way up the valley floor, tracking the stream bed. Still few cars.

In fact, it's cool. Yesterday's storms have split the seasons deftly in two: the oven that was August has given way to the clear crispness of September.

Now the ravine opens out into Gosau's high valley meadows and all at once, with all the theatrical drama of Richard Strauss' *Alpensymphonie*, the incredible rock backdrop of the Dachstein Massif hoves into view (I know *it* doesn't really move; *we* do ... but it *seems* to!) Even though I know it well, it never fails to overwhelm me. We stop for a short lunch break.

This is, without a doubt, one of the most picturesque places in Austria and the Gosau valley this autumn day is as close to paradise as we can get: the deep green velvet of carefully tended meadows cradling the jutting rock spires; the houses with hand-carved wooden balconies overflowing with crimson, yellow and orange flowers. Idyllic. Take away the roads and this scene would be the essence of serenity: a real world Shangri-la.

We turn off and follow the ever steeper road that takes us—with plenty of rest stops—the seven kilometers up to the two-tiered Gosau Lakes that mirror the Dachstein's summit in their perfectly calm waters. We're bushed and it's such a lovely spot that we stop for supper on an open terrace to drink in this panorama. Jean is already there, having a spritely "G'spritzer".

Enough mountain cycling for today! After supper, we load our bikes and ourselves into the car, then we retrace our route and return to Gosau for the night in a simple bed and breakfast. It takes all of about three seconds to fall asleep with the windows wide open.

Next morning's more leisurely. After breakfast we follow Hwy 166 through the Lammertal's unfolding vistas to Annaberg and, circling the Dachstein massif, on to Filzmoos, the doorway to the mountain's south side. From there we continue 13 km uphill towards the Ramsau and, before it, the entrance to the Dachstein Panorama Road. John insists on cycling but my thighs say no alpine biking for today so Jean and I drive; after all, somebody has to deliver the car!

This scenic toll road, with its six kilometers and seven hairpin turns, takes us up 500 meters in elevation, from 1,200m to 1,700m, delivering us to the foot of the Dachstein Glacier cable car that will transport us up to the ice field itself, perched at 2,700m.

With each passing minute and meter of altitude, the jagged, craggy Dachstein South Face emerges more dramatically. It seems to possess a force field of its own, the vast expanse of its sheer rock, wrinkled like steel grey crêpe, reaching across the valley and drawing us like surfers sucked under the crest of its huge petrified wave.

But we keep driving and finally, at the top of the tree line, reach the cable car station. We park the car and get three tickets for the exhilarating 1,000 vertical meter ascent (1,700 – 2,700m) to the Alps' easternmost glacier. After quite a wait for John to turn up (he's had his exercise for the day!), we have lunch, load his bike and set off on foot with our hiking boots for the Dachstein Seilbahn.

As we are swept effortlessly upward by the cable car, along with another 70 or so nature lovers, we see the hikers on the trail to the South Face hut (1,871m) as tiny as toys. Not a word of English is to be heard; everyone's speaking German. But the "Ooohs! and "Aahs!" need no translation when our cable car, suspended freely over the 2,700m of distance between the bottom and top stations, approaches the sheer rock face at about a 40° angle, bringing it almost close enough to reach out and touch! Then we glide effortlessly up the last meters, my ears popping with the altitude, and "dock." Whew!

A little light-headed with the sudden altitude, we head for the panorama terrace for what I remember as an incredible vista of snow and ice—but what a shock! How it's melted! Under this summer's scorching 40° C sun, the Dachstein Glacier is ***global warming personified***. It's devastating to see the ghastly glacier cracks—yawning crevasses, really—where pristine snowfields used to be. Now the whole surface is covered with a mixture of sooty moraine and Saharan sand whose dark color makes the ice melt even faster. Looking at the outdoor thermometer, I see it registers 9° C even at 2,700 meters! No wonder everything's melting.

So no more year-round glacier skiing. The T-bar lift is stranded in gravel. As for the cross-country and biathlon training tracks used by the Austrian Olympic team and others, though the main one is now non-existent, heroic efforts have been made to rescue the few remnants of snow: we see only six tracks—pearl white necklace loops in the solemn gray expanse—and no one's skiing.

For alpinists, too, this is a tragedy. There used to be a wide, well-marked track over to the upper Dachstein nanatuk rocks jutting out of the glacier, permitting an easy half-day ascent of this 3,004m peak. But now there's only bare, dirty ice full of dangerous, gaping black holes.

So no glacier promenade for us today. Instead, we sun ourselves on the terrace, share a bowl of Fritattensuppe (broth with fine cut pancake strips and chives), and reminisce about the better pre-environmental havoc days. Sitting there in the sun, I tell Jean and John the story of my first encounter with a mountain: it was right here on the Dachstein!

The Dachstein: Encountering My First Mountain

Mid-August 1967. Everything was different then. Not only was I four decades younger (and 40 lbs lighter!), our Dachstein ascent was definitely not from this side of the mountain—the notoriously sheer South Face! My first encounter with mountaineering was nevertheless unforgettable!

It was mid-July and we—the five of us, foreign students from Vienna University's Strobl am Wolfgangsee summer campus, plus our two Austrian faculty guides, Kurt and Heinz—hiked up via the Krippenstein at the far end of the Hallstättersee on a pristine five-hour traverse of the high-plateau 'Am Stein' that brought us at last to the landmark Simonyhütte (2,206m). The day was hot and crystal clear with breathtaking 360° panorama views of nearby summits and lakes. We would spend the night in this alpine hut and climb the Dachstein at daybreak next morning. Anticipation!

New York-born Texan that I was, this was my first night ever in an alpine hut. I was immediately impressed by the no-nonsense weathered wood and fist-thick steel cables attached to the roof and riveted into the rock slab where it stood. In contrast, I was also taken with the air of relaxed camaraderie the hut exuded. And no wonder. Each of the 20 or so hikers who would share this space tonight was "special" in that each had gotten here under his/her own steam; there was no easy, automatic access; our physical exertion was our entry fee.

After leaning against a warm rock wall, soaking in the sun's late afternoon rays, the air began to turn nippy and we went inside, which I found even more delightful. The quaintness of little details like the red-and-white checkered curtains, the rough-hewn wooden tables and floors, the enticing aroma of a steaming "Bergsteigersuppe" (mountain climbers' pea soup with wurst), and finally my first amazed sight of the "Matrazenlager," a huge room with wall-to-wall mattresses where would all sleep together(!), wrapped in sleeping bags or scatchy wool blankets, side by side, as if we had known each other forever.

We'd had such a perfect hiking day without a cloud in the sky that I was giddy with excitement over my very first real mountain expedition. The Dachstein's summit—actually a nanatuk of rock protruding through the glacial ice—was still hiding out of sight behind the steep snowfield we would ascend next morning. Like children on Christmas Eve, we went to bed … but this time there was no Santa Claus.

Instead, in the middle of the black-shrouded night, I was jolted awake by an incredible storm. Gusts of wind rattled the windows and when I looked out, what did I see but a snowstorm—in the middle of summer! In this howling wind and swirling snow, the hut trembled so I feared that we would be swept away any instant. Remembering those steel cables, I prayed they would hold.

"Oh, no! No mountain," I wailed to myself. Unable to sleep, I got up and tiptoed in stocking feet down to the communal kitchen. Who was there but Kurt, our guide (with whom I was quite taken), sipping tea as peaceful as could be. "What's going to happen to our tour in this awful weather?" I asked.

"One thing we learn in the mountains is that many things like the weather are beyond our control," he said, smiling at me. "Another is patience … let's just wait and see." I marveled at his calmness. And wait and see, we did, for another three hours. Still, the storm stayed. Though the wind died down, the snow fell even thicker, big white flakes like Christmas pastries.

Finally, though, we had to go. "We won't be able to do the summit in this storm," Kurt said. "It's a rock climb at the end; it will be cold and icy and you all haven't any alpine experience. So we'll have to cross the snow ridge and go down the other side to where the second van is."

We were crestfallen but what could we say? He was right. So we put on every stitch of clothing we had brought, including caps, gloves, anoraks and glacier glasses to protect against glare in this white-out. Then Kurt and Heinz roped the five of us together and we set off. Sinking knee-deep into the new snow, we struggled up the snowfield and crossed its flank at a 30° angle, taking several hours to reach what seemed to be a ridge next to a steep rock face.

Visibility was virtually zero. Without explanation, Kurt began helping us into full climbing harnesses, then clipping us into the rope with carabiners. We were huddled against this sheer rock wall and couldn't see more than five meters in any direction.

I figured we would now start down and so was surprised when Kurt turned around, grabbed a metal ring, which I hadn't even noticed jutting out of the wall, and began climbing lithely up the all but vertical rock face, disappearing almost instantly into the snowstorm.

Soon I heard a muffled, "Nachkommen. Follow me," followed by a tug on the rope clipped to my harness at chest level. "Who, me?" flitted through my mind but, next thing I knew, there I was, scrambling up that rock, then another, yet another, finding ledges for my feet and wet rocks or the occasional metal ring for my hands to pull myself up. Reaching the rock platform where Kurt was standing, I watched as he belayed the others. "Wow, some ridge," I thought to myself after another 45 minutes of this, "wonder what the real summit would've been like…"

We did one more rope length and, just as I clambered ungracefully on hands and knees onto an icy ledge and stood up, Kurt grinned and said, "Berg heil! You've just climbed the Dachstein!"

"I have?" I asked, looking around through the streaming snow and fog. True, I couldn't see anything jutting up any higher. "But I thought this was the ridge."

> *"We didn't want to spoil your first 3000'er just because of a little snow,"*
> *Kurt said, "but you'll have to do it again one day when the weather's*
> *better."*
>
> *... and that I did. But only some 30 years later for this particular peak.*
> *Still, the Dachstein is the one that got me started, my initial encounter*
> *with mountain climbing à la autrichienne. In the interim years, I*
> *immersed myself in this magic, scaling the highest peaks in Austria,*
> *Switzerland and several other countries. Almost every summer and*
> *autumn weekend for years!*
>
> *Mountain climbing is addictive—but not deadly as many who have*
> *never tried it assume—so long as you have patience, take exceptional*
> *care with everything under your control and remember that a lot of it*
> *isn't under your control—60% of alpine weather is not good—and*
> *just do it anyway. Mountaineering has remained one of Austria's most*
> *precious gifts to me.*

******

So, to finish this saga, when at last I came back to do the Dachstein by beautiful weather, it was with my UN colleague and long-time mountaineering buddy, Lubor, in the summer of 1998. We "cheated" by using this new cable car—but then climbed a more difficult variation of the normal route, the Northwest Ridge along the shoulder. A three-hour climb with breathtaking panoramic views until five minutes before the summit when—guess what?! A big black cloud swept in and, between thunder and bolts of lightening—dumped buckets of hail on us as we clung to the summit cross that vibrated with electricity; then quickly slid down ice-clad gullies and a steep snow ridge to the normal glacier return route. So typical! Lubor and I took one look at each other ... and laughed out loud! Weather in the mountains—as fickle and unpredictable as a teenage romance—and every bit as exciting, too!

Ramsau reflections

Now we're back at an idyllic pension (bed and breakfast) in the Ramsau where, before leaving on the next leg of our journey, I take a walk through the larch forest to a small lake with a vacated summer cottage beside it.

It reminds me of an afternoon once shared here with someone very special. We had walked this same path in fall, on a soft bed of newly fallen larch needles, arrived at the cottage where we took refuge there from a sudden rainstorm. An architect, he drew me a little sketch of the place flanked by the towering trees.

I still have it, framed, as a reminder. I also have the strange little bit of wood we found while walking back, a piece broken off from something larger on which was written, "Nach zwanzig Jahren"—"in twenty years." Since I left Austria in 1988, it has now been just about that.

The Inner Salzkammergut: After breakfast the next morning, we take a scenic ride on one of the historic piroges-like boats that ply the Hallstättersee and recall the Pfingsten Boat Festival in May of each year. After that, it's time for John to return to Vienna while I make my way alone up to the Gosausee.

Taking a car this time—this is steep territory—I drive up the curving, narrow road which follows a ravine, arriving in the early evening stillness on the high plateau where the town of Gosau forms three separate clusters—vordere, mittel und hintere (front, middle and back) Gosau—in the otherwise unspoiled green meadowlands. Towering above this gentle valley are the turrets and towers of the Gosaukamm, a forbidding rock ridge that etches itself into the evening sky.

Stopping for the night at the family-run Gosauerhof, I leave my things in the room and go back downstairs for a leisurely dinner on the outdoor terrace. Of course, the whole Salzkammergut is hunting country, ennobled by the fact that Emperor Franz Josef came to these parts every single year to do just that. And so, as a dinner treat, I choose the Rehmedallions mit Rotkraut und Preiselbeeren—deer medallions with red cabbage and cranberries.

❖ **Deer Medallions with green pepper sauce and red cabbage**

Ingredients:
1 ¾ lbs roe deer back
½ lb celeriac
1 ¾ oz. butter
3 ½ oz. cream
3 ½ oz. chanterelle mushrooms
3 ½ oz. cepe mushrooms
1 shallot
3 ¼ c. red wine
¾ c. apple juice
2 ¾ T port wine
½ lb. red cabbage
1 laurel leaf
1 branch thyme
1 branch rosemary

For the sauce:
1 T. green pepper
1 c. cream
½ lb. vegetables (broccoli, carrots)
3 pt. roe deer stock (fond)
1 laurel leaf
1 branch thyme
1 branch rosemary

Preparation: Take the roe deer back fillets. Remove the back tendons. They will be used for the sauce later on. Cut the meat into medallions. Tie the medallions with a kitchen string so that they keep a nice form. Count about 3 roe deer medallions per person. Salt and pepper the two sides. Sear each side for about 2 minutes. Then, take them out off the pan, where you put the already prepared tendons.

Add the vegetables as well as the herbs. The whole has to be very well seared for about 10 minutes until you obtain a nice colour. Then, sprinkle the red wine over it. Reduce the red wine and add the roe deer fond, which has been refined with the roe deer bone. Thus, you can prepare it 2-3 days in advance. Add the crème fraiche (heavy cream) and let it simmer in the pan for about 10 minutes.

While the sauce cooks calmly, take a frying pan and put the green pepper inside. Then, pour the roe deer sauce over the green pepper, using a sieve. Let it encore reduce until it seems good for you. Cut the red cabbage into very thin slices. Next, lay it in a marinade of red wine and apple juice. Add thyme, laurel, spices, port-wine, and sugar. After all this has been marinated well, cook for 2-3 hours. The cabbage will caramelize with the sugar and turn tender afterwards.

For the garnishing, you need celery puree. Peel the root and cut it into dice. Finally, cook it in a mix of milk and creme fraiche (same proportions each), until it is very, very tender. Put the whole in a mixer and add some butter to this puree. Salt and pepper.

Put butter in a pan and add the hacked mushrooms, the chanterelles as well as the cepe mushroom heads. At the end of the cooking, add salt and chervil. Place a cepe mushroom head on top of each medallion. Sprinkle with bread crumps and put it in the oven at 302 degrees F for 6-7 minutes.

Place the red cabbage, then the chanterelles and the celery puree on a serving dish. Withdraw the medallions from the oven and put them on the serving dish. Add the broccoli pieces, the sauteed carrots, and, to finish, pour the sauce over it. **Bon apétit!**

Afternoon turns into evening and, as I take in the panorama from my dining terrace, I jot down a few haiku poems to capture the transformation.

> *cotton candy spires—*
> *soft clouds crown rock-hard turrets*
> *Gosaukamm halo*

night falls, spikes soften
ridges dissolve in darkness
as day becomes dreams

The night is brilliantly clear and star-studded. Next morning I get up at dawn to drive up to one of my very favorite places: the Gosausee, actually a series of glacial lakes that capture the run-off of the Alps' easternmost glacier and, at the same time, preserve a mood of serenity.

By 0800 I'm already up at the valley head, have parked the car and embarked all alone on the trail that runs around the lower lake. This famously photographed Vordere Gosausee that mirrors the Dachstein Massf in its five kilometer-circumference frame, is a transparent bottle-green hue, almost 100m deep and encircled with firs and deciduous trees. A prehistoric feeling pervades.

Amazing to find oneself alone on such a magnificent day: perfectly clear, sunny and promising to be hot. Setting off around the right side of the lake, the meadows are still pearled with dew. Light and shadow split the mirror-still lake into twin images. Nothing moves but me. Cool air. Warm sunshine. Immobile cloudless sky.

I reach the halfway point around the lake in less than half an hour and now the "less traveled road"—an hour's additional hike to the Hintere Gosausee (the upper lake)—beckons me. I take it, drawn to see for myself this high lake that catches the direct run-off from the fast-dissolving Dachstein glacier. Even comparing with a recent postcard, it's clear: what was once white glacier is now gray moraine.

Much steeper than the first trail, this one leads up on a gravel path through sun-dappled shade, shaded green. Climbing high, through thick woods, past moss-embossed boulders, I pass a series of small lakes, some pristine, some brackish, beneath the sheer slate cliffs of the Gosaukamm that now towers directly above me. Labouring upwards in the morning stillness and rising heat, I finally reach the crest. Below me is my goal: the highest lake. Secluded in the sunshine. No signs of civilization save a single, solitary "Almhütte" at the far end of the lake. But there are no rushing waterfalls either as I had imagined. Instead stillness.

As I circle the lake's right bank towards the steep trail that veers off to the Dachstein's Adamek Hut three hours up, I catch sight of one couple who perhaps just came down or else camped overnight. Now they sit together in a clearing at the water's edge. As I watch while walking, the red-sweatered girl rises, slowly strips off her hiking clothes and, nude-secluded, dips into the lake. Like Eve in paradise. Enchanted, I continue on my way.

Finally, three-and-a-half hours and about 500 meters in altitude up and down—the lower and upper lakes lie at 930m and 1,154m respectively—find me back at the now teeming tourist point at the main Gosausee. From here, the oft-photographed scene emerges: the symmetrical view of the pristine green lake, its three wooded flanks on either side, followed by bizarre nanatuk rock formations that thrust themselves through the Dachstein glacier.

But the majesty is no match for the minutaie here where shops and stands hawk everything from postcards and salt candles to something more unusual: marmot salve. As I replenish my liquid deficit after that hot hike, the following placard distracts me from my refreshing "G'spritzer" (white wine mixed with mineral water). Irreverently translated (including a bit of poetic license) below, it reads more or less as follows:

"Whistle a Happy Tune …": Marmot Salve for Sore Muscles:

Our mountain marmots, which are also known for their cheerful, high-pitched whistle, live wild in Nature but have become very important for the local inhabitants. Especially their body fat is rich is physical-chemical qualities for healing. In autumn, marmot fat is pure white, only about 10-12% water, and contains valuable nutrients from the high alpine vegetation that comprise the marmots' diet: moss, ferns, leaves, flowers and roots, all of which are rich in vitamins D and E.

Our traditional local marmot salve (only €15/bottle) cures everything from vertebral disc pain to gicht, arthritis, frost contusions, rheumatism, arm, leg and joint pains (whatever you haven't got, it'll give it to you!").

Use it twice a day for 21 days, then stop for awhile. You will notice the difference after only a few days. Then you can "whistle a happy tune" like the locals do!

Taking stock of my aching knees after that steep descent, I decide to fall prey to the local lore and buy myself a bottle … at least it's aromatic. In silent homage to the deceased marmots who will henceforth contribute to relieving my various aches and pains, I rub it in …

Meanwhile, at the tour bus pour-out place, German stride about, clonking their Nordic walking sticks on the concrete promenade, just as a horde of Japanese tourists, covered with sun hats, glasses, even gloves, spills out of their buses, instantly clicking away. Turning their back on the lake, the mountain and two gorgeously bronzed Austrian mountain bikers, they instead capture the shape of stolid houses. Then, clutching mobile phones for comfort, they climb back into their buses and are gone. Five-minute photo stop. No further comment.

Zell Am See: Alpine Site for All Seasons. A Sportsperson's Paradise:

Flying high and paragliding over alpine meadows, sailing on the Zellersee, summer skiing on the Kitzsteinhorn, mountain climbing, equestrian adventures.

Apple Strudel

Ingredients

7 oz flour, sifted	*1 egg, lightly beaten*	*1 T oil*
Pinch of salt	*3 oz (173 cup) water*	

Filling:

3 oz raisins	*2 T rum*	*2 oz butter, softened*
3 ½ lbs cooking apples	*4 oz sugar*	*pinch of cinnamon*
3-4 oz (1/2 c.) bread crumbs	*3 T powdered sugar (decoration)*	
4 oz butter, softened		

Dough: *Sift the flour into a bowl. Make a depression in the middle and drop in the egg, oil and salt. Add water gradually while slowly beating the dough until it forms a medium-firm ball. Knead by hand for 10 min. more until the dough has a silky sheen. Let stand about 30 min.*

Filling: *Drizzle rum over the raisins and let them stand. Peel and seed the apples, then slice them thinly. Stir in cinnamon and sugar.*

Spread a clean tablecloth or sheet on a large table. Sprinkle with flour and roll the dough out as thin as possible. Stretch the dough gently from the center outwards, using the backs of your hands, lightly clenched, palms down, moving around the table. Cut off the thicker edges and use to patch if necessary.

Preheat the oven to 400-425 degrees F. Grease a baking sheet. Sprinkle bread crumbs on the dough. Cover 2/3 of the dough with apple filling and raisins. Fold the sides of the dough in over filling. Using the cloth, gently roll the dough over itself, jelly-roll fashion, until the filling is enclosed. Use the cloth to slide the strudel onto the baking sheet. Baste with melted butter. Bake for 45-55 min., basting occasionally with butter. Dust with powdered sugar and serve. **Bon apétit!**

As the travel prospect promises, "the only thing you *won't* be in the Europa Sportregion Zell am See/Kaprun is *bored*." And it's true! Besides just hanging out—what the Austrians poetically call, "mit der Seele bäumeln"—this is a sporty person's paradise with no less than twenty activities to keep one busy, rain or shine.

- On land, there's walking, running, biking, hiking, climbing, skiing and snowboarding; oh yes, and also tennis, golf and riding;

- On water, there's swimming, sailing, wind-surfing, water-skiing and diving; oh yes, and also rafting and canyoning;

- On/in air, there paragliding, parachuting and flying … and "high ropes". Hmmm.

But it's more than just a hyperactivist's dream. What actually brings me back here time and again is the sheer beauty of the place. Even as I write this, I'm sitting on a balcony overlooking the deep blue Zellersee that is four km long by one km wide, almost 70 meters deep, boasts "drinking quality water" in summer and ice skating/sailing quality in winter.

After breakfast I saunter down to the Hotel Bellevue's private dock to be picked up by the brand new *Schmittenhöhe* passenger boat, recently commissioned, that will take me on a ten minute ride across to Zell am See that hugs the far shore under the mountain's shadow. This town was known to the Romans and named "Cella in Bisonzio" by monks from

Salzburg in the 8th century. At that time, granted, its scenic beauty was less important than its strategic location on the trade route over the Alps to the south. Today that route has become the **Großglockner High Alpine Road**, Austria's highest drivable pass that connects the province of Salzburg to that of East Tyrol and Austria to Italy.

For now though, my gaze wanders westward where the **Kitzsteinhorn** pushes its snow-clad peak above the clouds. At over 3,000m, this is the first summer ski region to have been made accessible by cable car in 1965 and was at the time regarded as a "revolutionary" technological masterpiece. Ten years before, the Tauernkraftwerk did some equally audacious building in the form of an enormous dam to create two tiered artificial lakes that provide hydroelectric energy, as well as hiking trails high above the village of Kaprun.

Since Zell am See got together with Kaprun in the late 1960s to form the **Europa Sportregion**, the area has flourished. In the early 1970s, I vividly recall the excitement of my first visit to Zell, Kaprun and the Kitzsteinhorn for summer skiing—and I mean to revive that memory now!

Well, I *meant* to, but though open most of the year, the Kitzsteinhorn is closed just now for renovations. Now mid-afternoon on the first bright day after two chilly, rainy ones on the Zellersee and everyone, including me, is eager to hit the mountain trail again.

So, on the spur of the moment, I decide to explore a place I've long heard about but never been: the heart of the **High Tauern National Park**, highlights of which are the two high-alpine artificial reservoirs created by the Kaprun Hydroelectric Power Plant. Although these two azure blue lakes beckon, access is not so simple from here. I have to drive up to the "staging area," where private vehicles are parked, and then embark on a mini-odyssey that involves two specially equipped buses and, linking them, the world's biggest open-air diagonal lift, which transports passengers and heavy equipment at a maximum incline of 80%—that's right, all but vertical!

At the top, I walk across the top of the dam, then head for a thread-thin trail along the far flank of the lake that looks totally deserted. Not that there aren't hordes of summer tourists, but they flock only as far as the first observatory deck before succumbing to the temptation of yet another "Kaffee und Kuchen."

Not me. Not yet anyway. First I'm going to follow the trail that skirts the left side of the upper lake. It takes almost two hours, during which time I cross six rushing waterfalls but see only six people. Incredible!

At 3:00 PM I find myself blissfully alone, sitting on a sun-warmed boulder and dipping my bare toes into the liquid ice that is the melt water running off the Pasterze Glacier barely 500 meters away. It looms above me, hanging over a steep black shiny rock face, spewing out cascades into half a dozen deep ravines. They all come together to form the rushing torrent that sweeps past my feet as I sit on my boulder at the far end of the lake where it all starts and marvel at the unspoiled, untouched majesty of it all. The sound of water is like 100 high-pressure fire hoses.

Actually *glad* not to see another living soul. A very precious, personal moment.

Starting back only around 3:30, the trail is still drenched in sunlight … but totally deserted. It occurs to me that I totally forgot to ask when the last trip down was. So I get a move on, re-cross all six waterfalls, five of which have a tiny four-slat bridge without handholds, one of which has apparently been washed away altogether. Now pressed for time, I make my way back, encountering no one and arrive, slightly breathless, just in time to catch the very last bus down. Aahhh!

****

OCTOBER: The Wachau And The Beautiful Blue Danube

The Wachau. *This picturesque area is part of the legendary Danube Valley that carries this swiftly flowing, second longest river in Europe from its source in Germany's Black Forest through Vienna, then Budapest, Belgrade and at last into the Black Sea, passing altogether through eight countries.*

Only in Austria can you find such friendly landlords! At least that's my experience after having lived in many different countries. Mine are

Hilde and Michael Pfeffer. Both Austrian-born, he's a superb example of the "Species Gemütlicher Wiener"—easy-going Viennese—and gourmet cook, while she's a dynamo of entrepreneurial energy from Lower Austria, a province that includes Melk and the world-famous Wachau Wine region along the Danube.

One early autumn morning, they invite me (as they often do) for an all-day outing: first to Melk and then on to one of their favorite Wachau vintners, Gritsch (info@weingut-gritsch-wachau.at. Tel. 02713 22 08), in Spitz an der Donau. What starts out as a day trip ends up as a unique all-weekend experience when Rupert, the vineyard owner invites me to participate in the wine harvest.

Wachauer Wine Harvest

What strikes me first are his hands: working hands, dark under the nails and with fine-line scars on the cuticles. "Comes from working in the vineyards," Rupert says, "I already washed them twice. It's those *Blue Portuguese* grapes; the white ones don't leave such telltale colours."

The setting is Spitz an der Donau, a Rip van Winkle little village on the shores of the Danube and in the midst on one of Austria's supreme wine-growing districts: the Wachau. Sitting in the garden of Weingut Gritsch as evening falls, I gaze over at the golden-illuminated Hinterhaus castle ruin that ascends the hillside in four towered stages; just beyond it lies the Danube. We climbed up there just a few hours ago to bask in the afternoon's slanting sun and revel in the river's soft windings far below as she curves her way towards Vienna and on to the distant Black Sea. The castle used to be a fortress and has now been restored. People often stage weddings there, I'm told. A more romantic place would be hard to find! And what an exquisite home site it would make, this fairytale castle!

The tradition of homes, heritage and family are still very much alive and well in the Wachau so I ask Rupert about his family. "Although I was born here, the name 'Gritsch' isn't a local one," he says. "My family's roots are actually in South Tyrol" that used to be part of the Austrian Empire but belongs to Italy since the end of the First World War. "My wife Erika's family is long-term local though and so are most of the families around here who sometimes marry amongst themselves, keeping up that old Austrian tradition of romantic, rather than aggressive, acquisitions."

"Vineyards are the most valuable acquisitions around here. Today's Wachau has about 1,400 hectares of them—each hectare the equivalent of 10,000 square meters. About 220 of those belong to our village of Spitz where some 20 families are full-time wine producers and another 140 or so do it part-time. The town has about 30 Heuriger, half of them with guest rooms. Our own Gritsch vineyards comprise only about five hectares, some owned, some leased, scattered about these hills," he says, gesturing to the vineyard-rowed hills as far as the eye can see. "They include the picturesquely-named 'Tausendeimerberg' or 'Thousand-bucket Mountain.' As for us, we have a vacation apartment, four guest rooms, a sizeable garden and an indoor tavern but we're open—"Ausg'steckt' as they call it—only a total of about six weeks out of the year—10-15 days at a time between April and October."

Rupert and I get into one of those "existential" conversations. "You know, when I was a kid, my dream was to become a pilot, a *bush* pilot," he confesses, "but I guess I was too conscientious. When it turned out that I was to inherit this vineyard in 1980 from a distant relative who had no children, I took it, despite mixed feelings. Today the Weingut Gritsch measures five hectares—a proverbial "drop in the bucket" compared to the 1,400 hectares that make up all of the Wachau that stretches along the Danube between Melk and Krems. But it's enough to keep us busy all year 'round."

As for me, tonight I may be sitting in Rupert's cozy "Stube" sipping wine while chatting with him, but tomorrow I'll be busy hand-picking grapes all day long. Rupert tells me there are usually only 4-5 people but tomorrow we'll be eight because some others are coming to help … a little like an old-fashioned house-raising, I muse.

"We'll be picking only Grüner Veltiner," he says, glancing quickly at his fingernails in what I suspect may be an effort to re-assure me that mine won't look like his by tomorrow night. "But we'll have to hand-select. This year, because of the rain, a lot of grapes have gone bad and need to be tossed; can be we'll need to re-do the rows twice or even three times over a period of days or weeks … and you can't do *that* with machines. Of course, the Wachau vintners are known for *never* using machines anyway; we *always* hand-pick our grapes … that adds quality to the wine."

Pouring me another glass of smooth Grüner Veltliner, he lists off the features (besides hand-selecting) that make the Wachau wines so special. "Well, first, there's the *climate* that's influenced both by the Danube that stabilizes the temperature and by the Waldviertel (Forest quarter) to our north that keeps the nights cool and humid. Then there's the quality of the *soil* with its unique combination of sandy clay, gneiss and schist, plus the *angle of the slopes* to the sun. We're pretty much at the periphery of wine cultivation regions in terms of weather, but that can also work to our advantage" … especially if there's global warming, I think to myself, asking how far the harvest has already progressed.

"Right now, we're only about a quarter of the way into the grape harvest," Rupert tells me, saying that it usually takes six weeks or so—from the beginning of October to mid-November—to complete, with a few breaks in between and hoping that the weather holds. Startled by a photo collage on the wall dated October 27, 1997 that shows the vineyards covered in snow, I ask what that did to that year's wine harvest. "Nothing," Rupert says, "not at that stage. In the best case, you could have harvested 'ice wine' grapes afterwards … but the temperature would have had to drop to at least -7° C and it didn't." Somehow I'm relieved since today is already October 10th!

Yet another glass of white wine, this one a Neuburger with 12.5% alcohol, and the conversation warms up. I ask Rupert if he has kids who will take over the business from him one day. He says he has two sons and the eldest and heir apparent, Roman, has already done his apprenticeship in wine cultivation. "You know, the vineyards stay in our families for generations," Rupert says, "and not only that: until about 30 years ago, we Wachauers were totally self-sufficient." In his voice, I sense his pride in this achievement, together with what could be a tinge of nostalgia. And so I ask him—

"Tell me, Rupert, if your son took over the vineyards from you right now; if money were no object and you could travel anywhere you wanted, where would you go?" He looks slightly aghast at such a question but then his gaze goes skyward and he reels off without a moment's hesitation, "Australia, New Zealand, South America, the USA, Canada. Actually I was in Canada camping back in '78." And when I ask him why these particular places, he say, "The space ... that limitless space."

So with the limitless space of my dreams now calling, I bid good night to Rupert and my illuminated castle across the nippy-chilled night valley and drift off, wondering what tomorrow will bring ...

Wachauer Wine Harvest: The Experience

October morn after a night in the Gritsch's cozy little *pension* on its scenic vineyard-filled hillside overlooking Spitz an der Donau. Now my nose awakens to the subtle fragrance of fermenting grapes, floating on the chill air. No wonder. The harvest has been underway for two weeks now and the grapes are pressed right here in house!

Up, dressed and breakfasted in quick order, by 0800 I join today's grape harvesters in the orchard for our "picking orders." Today we're nine: "boss" Rupert and his twenty-something son Roman, Rupert's wife Erika, mother-in-law Hermine, neighbour Monika, cousin Ingrid with two friends, Hans and Anna, from Amstetten, and American me. It's a lively family potpourri with lots of peppery insider quips and conversation that give my spotty knowledge of local Austrian dialects a good workout.

Then Rupert gets down to business. "We're hand-selecting only Grüner Veltiner grapes today," he says, "let's start on these rows right up that hill." So, armed with our twenty-litre buckets, off we go up the hill right behind the house that is surrounded on three sides by vineyards.

Everything is covered in morning mist and dew, soon including my feet. Within five minutes, my nose is running and my hands, sticky wet from grape juice, are already feeling half-frozen. Still, no one's spirits are dampened. The weather forecast predicts we'll be more than warm by mid-morning. Still, when Ingrid asks me if I wouldn't like some gloves, I say yes, imagining mittens! Instead, what I get are a pair of thin white surgical gloves that, on the one hand, keep my fingers from sticking together and, on the other, might keep them from freezing ... or so I hope.

Soon I'm feeling like a displaced surgeon, my sheathed hand snipping away bunches of sweet Grüner Veltliner grapes with my bright orange clippers. We have picked two long horizontal rows of grapes, and as we move along them, people pepper up the morning with their spritely chatter, jokes, local gossip and laughter. This outgoing attitude is typically Austrian and one of the things that most endears them to my heart.

Still, my visions of a grape-like Garden of Eden are quickly dashed. Instead, we have to stringently select amongst the "Grapes of (Rain's) Wrath"! Working as carefully as our surgeon's gloves would suggest, we make incisions in the closely packed clusters to snip out and discard the damaged parts, dropping the rest into our buckets that Roman collects and empties into the tractor-drawn container every so often.

Just two 50-metre-long rows take us an entire morning. Entire damaged grape clusters have to be discarded. Appalled, I ask Rupert about the yield and he says, "Our five hectares usually yields about 6,000 litres of wine per hectar; but this year we'll be lucky if we get 3,500. Still, all the more reason to select with care. That way, even if we don't have as much in *quantity*, the *quality* won't suffer." By the time we stop for lunch at noon, we have just about filled a single 350-kg container, far from the usual three. But that doesn't mean we're any less hungry so around twelve, we knock off and walk down to the house for an abbreviated version of the *Hauer Jause* "working lunch":

"Vintner's Snack"

The Wachau is known for its authentic, homemade Hauer Jause consisting of pork-based cold cuts, such as those featured below, served on an amply round wooden platter, together with cheese, condiments and quantities of newly harvested white 'heuriger' wine leavened with tasty dark rye-wheat bread and/or rolls (e.g. Wachauer Leiberl, Salzstangerl, Kornspitz):

Verhackteres (Minced pork)	**Geselchtes (Smoked pork)**
Geselchtes Bauchfleisch faschiert	
Gemischt und gewurzt	**Karrée** rucken von halben Schwein
Grammelschmalz (Lard)	**Hauer Blunzen (Blood sausage)**
Uncooked bacon, cubed	Pork parts (tongue, head, no brain)
Pan warmed, fat poured off	Pork blood + parts mixed
Re-warmed and pressed (fat squeezed out)	Pork intestines as sausage skin
Garlic added and	Cooked, then served cold with
Served on dark, toasted bread	Mustard, horseradish and applesauce
Liptauer and Frühlingsstreichkäse	Caraway roast

Spicy-sharp accessories: Pfefferoni, freshly shredded horseradish, marinated cocktail onions and mini-cornichons (pickles)

Since it's only midday and we've got lots of work ahead, there's juice and water instead of wine to go with our "snack," but, to compensate, Erika brings out a sweet-tooth's delight for dessert—apricot torte and round poppyseed tarts. Meanwhile, the weather's gotten deliciously warm so we eat outside on picnic tables. The mood is jovial and relaxed with lots of local chatter (and not a word of world politics!) and, in a little over half an hour, are back in the vineyards, this time at a better location.

After this morning's experience, we're relieved that these two rows of Grüner Veltliner grapes a bit lower down the slope have better weathered the rain's wrath. Here are entire clusters of absolutely perfect grapes, lovely to look at and deliciously sweet to the taste.

It's really nice and warm now—a perfect autumn day—and before long, I find myself in a state of mild euphoria, clipping these perfect grape clusters, tasting a few every so often, and filling my bucket with ease compared to this morning. By the time it's finally time to stop at five o'clock, I've gotten myself into such a meditative state that I think I could go on forever. The grapes are as perfect as the day and spread before me, row upon row in the afternoon sun, like one of those rare and wonderful dreams of abundance, now become reality.

No matter that everything is sticky sweet—from hands to hair, from shirtsleeves to jeans—from this "ambrosia of the gods." That's part of our reward for a long day's work.

This rest of our reward comes as the evening meal to which we are invited as more than ample reimbursement for our sun-kissed hours in the vineyards. Erika has whipped up a traditional Austrian dinner: tender pork roast, potato dumplings and cole slaw, washed down with a Grüner Veltiner *Federspiel* from this very vineyard and followed by yet more apricot torte and poppyseed tarts. Being such a good cook, when I ask her for the recipes, she looks at me with a slightly puzzled look, then says, "Oh, I never use a cookbook; just do it all intuitively, with "finger-tip feeling"; thus, the Spitz-appropriate title, *Schweinsbraten nach FingerSPITZen gefühl*" below:

Erika's "Schweinsbraten nach FingerSPITZengefühl" mit Kartoffelknödel und Krautsalat
(Erika's Pork Roast with Potato Dumplings and Austrian Cole Slaw)

Ingredients (4 Servings):

1 kg Pork roast carrée
1-2 cloves garlic
Salt and pepper
1 onion sliced, 2 T caraway seeds

In the past, pork was provided by local farmers; now it comes from the supermarket. Pick a lean cut of pork, rub in salt, pepper and caraway seeds. Place in a baking pan with the garlic and onion slices in about 1-2 centimeters of water in the bottom. Roast at 200ºC in an electric convection oven for about two hours. Serve piping hot with its own au jus *clear natural juice gravy.*

Potato dumplings (4 Servings):

1 kg floury potatoes (not "kipfler" salad potatoes)

Salt, 1 T semolina

30-40 dkg griffiges flour (depending on the potatoes)

1 egg

Cook potatoes with skin in boiling water. Peel them hot and pass through a strainer to make them light and fine. Fold in the salt, Grieß and flour and, with wet hands, knead the mixture into four dumplings. Drop them into salted boiling water and cook uncovered until they rise to the surface. Remove and serve warm.

Austrian Cole Slaw (Krautsalat) (4 Servings):

1 head of white cabbage (ca. 1 kg)	*Salt, caraway seeds,*
1 part oil : 5 parts vinegar : few drops water	*Pinch of sugar (to dilute the sharp vinegar)*

Season to taste.

Slice the cabbage into thin strips, mix in the salt and caraway seeds. Let stand for 5-6 hours to soften the cabbage. Then sprinkle a pinch of sugar over the mixture, adding oil, followed by water-thinned vinegar. Mix and serve crisp-chilled.

Wine: Wachauer Federspiel (Grüner Veltliner) from Wine Cellar Gritsch

Guten appetit!

Talk now turns to the wines themselves, since these vineyards are both famous and historic. The Wachau lies on the 48th latitude, right on the outermost northern limits of the world's wine-growing regions … but its micro-climate makes all the difference. First of all, there's the contrast between the warm days and cool nights that create a "seesaw" (i.e. Wechselspiel) between the Danube Valley's temperate climate and the Waldviertel's pine-spicy-icy-cold "blue northers". Then there's the Danube itself that plays a mediating influence, reflecting and thus magnifying the sun's relatively scarce rays in this part of the northern hemisphere. This combination, it is claimed, imbues the wine grapes with a very special bouquet.

The Romans hit upon this heady combination as long ago as the 5th century, according to local Spitz historian, Erich Schöner. And after Charlemagne ousted the Hun invaders at the end of the 8th century, the Catholic Church assumed an ever more central role. When the Benedictines arrived to build their monasteries in the 9th century, the Church encouraged wine cultivation from the Middle Ages onwards. The name "Wachau" first appears in an 823 proclamation while the name Spitz is first mentioned in the year 870 in connection with the conversion of the Bavarians … As one sees in travelling through the Wachau, the Church was omnipresent in those days.

Long Grass, Falcons and Lizards—What have *They* to do with Wine? A Lot!

Now let's take a closer look at the truly enchanting Wachau wines. Just as, once upon a time in the 13-14th century, King Leuthold I von Kuenring saw fit to anoint the region between Melk and Krems with the august title, ***Vinea Wachau Nobilis Districtus—Wachau, Noble Wine Region***—so in the 20th century, the Wachau Winegrowers' Association took the initiative to re-introduce this title, as well as its regional wine "protectorate," updating it through the creation of three categories of fully natural (i.e. unadulterated) wines uniquely associated with the Wachau:

- **Steinfeder:** This label refers to the *stipa pennata* (i.e. soft, **long grass**) of the Wachau's steep wine terraces and was launched in 1984 to take in those light Wachauer wines with maximum 11% alcohol content that nevertheless have complex fruity aromas, nuances and class;

- **Federspiel:** The name, "feather game," comes from the Wachau's once popular falconry and refers to the way in which the **falcon** was enticed to return to alight on its owner's gloved hand. Like the falcon, this classic dry white wine exhibits a racy elegance and up to 12.5% alcohol content;

- **Smaragd:** This, the highest quality (and strongest) Wachau wine, takes it name from the emerald-hued **lizard** often found sunning itself on the warm vineyard-steeping rocks. With an alcohol content of minimum 12.5%, it is a full-bodied, yet racy, white wine, like a Lipizzaner thoroughbred horse in the world of wine-breeding.

Let's take a closer look at Austria's wines and what to eat with them with since it is well-known fact that regional specialties are best complimented by their very own local wines:

Dish/Type of Food	Recommended Austrian Wine	Wine Attributes
Aperitifs, tapas	Dry sparkling wine	Effervescent, refreshing
Shellfish	Grüner Veltliner, Rheinriesling	Sparkling-fresh; Elegant and nervy
Freshwater fish	Grüner Veltliner, Rheinriesling	Sparkling-fresh; Elegant and nervy
Freshwater fish, broiled	Pinot Blanc,	
Barrique-Chardonnay		
Fruity, full-bodied		
Ocean fish	Welschriesling	Sparkling-fresh
Ocean fish, broiled	Pinot Blanc	
Omelet	Pinot Blanc	
Coldcut platter	Blauburgunder, Schilcher	Fruity and velvety; light and elegant
Dark meat (beef, lamb)	Blauburgunder,	
Blaufränkisch	Fruity, velvety	

Light, fruity		
White meat (veal, pork)	Weißburgunder, Welschriesling, Schilcher	Full-bodied; Sparkling-fresh;
light and elegant		
Fowl (chicken)	Neuburger	Fruity and full-bodied
Fowl, dark meat (duck, goose, turkey)	Portugieser Rotweine	Light and mild
Fowl (Wild)	Blauburgunder	Fruity and velvety
Game	Blauburgunder, Blaufränkisch, auch Spätlese	Fruity and velvety; Light and fruity; Sweeter, more full-bodied
Cheese platter, mild	Welschriesling, Silvaner, Blauer Portugieser	Sparkling-fresh; Spicy, aromatic;
Light and mild		
Cheese, spicy	Strong Blaufränkisch, Zweigelt	Full-bodied fruity; Light and mild
Cake, tart, pie	Ruster Ausbruchweine, Traminer Auslese	Noble-sweet; Spicy, aromatic and full-bodied
Fruit (peaches, strawberries, nuts)	Ruländer, Traminer, Tokaje	Full with body; Spicy and aromatic

Source: Freude am Wein, Susi Piroué, 2004.

NOVEMBER: Ötschergräben: The "Grand Canyon" Of Austria

Only a short, scenic two hours from Vienna, the 154 km² Ötscher Gorge is the biggest national park in this region and is locally known as the "Grand Canyon of Austria." It reminds us of a wild West movie with its deep gorge and bizarre dolomite rock formations. And while "Grand Canyon" may be a bit of hyperbole, this hike is one of my favorites, lying as it does on Vienna's geographic doorstep.

Lubor, my Czech-born Bergkamerad on dozens of hikes and climbs over the years, and I decide to revisit this remarkable place. We've been here before to do a longer tour up the 'Rauher Kamm'—the 'raw ridge' on the right side that leads to the summit of the Ötscher. This time though we'll just do the gorge.

We plan to arise with the dawn and be on site before the Sunday strollers and Indian summer heat gets too intense. But the night before was another of those delightful evenings spent sipping new wine in the outdoor garden of a nearby heuriger—those charming wine taverns utterly unique to Vienna and their heady "three-quarter time wines," new wines made from the most recent grape harvest. Small surprise that the dawn arose without us. No matter. Half a day is plenty of time for this excursion.

After a leisurely breakfast, off we drive, first over the Höhenstrasse that weaves through the Vienna Woods to the west of the city and then onto the Westautobahn, the main superhighway linking Vienna with points west like Linz and Salzburg. But we're not going that far. After half an hour, we turn off and start winding our way south through the velvet green hillsides abloom with wildflowers, especially buttercups and bright red poppies. Fragrant, freshly cut meadows alternate with ripening fields of grain and corn, making a green and golden patchwork quilt below the tree-topped hillsides. Our small two-lane road follows alongside the meandering Traisen River. Geranium-bedecked balconies and gable-roofed houses with vegetable gardens greet us as we glide through this idyllic valley.

Soon we reach Lilienfeld—"Lilies of the Field"—which consists mainly of the enormous Baroque monastery for which it was named. Then we pass through the village of Türnitz and climb the serpentine ribbon of road up to Annaberg. This village with its black-spired onion dome commands a splendid view over the Ötscher Valley and mountain peak before us. Amazingly, there are almost no cars; we have this paradise all to ourselves.

We descend now to Wienerbruck where we park the car, put on our day packs and set off along a sun-dappled, deeply wooded trail. All is quiet, save the muffled sound of water that gets louder the closer we approach.

Suddenly, as we round a corner, the panorama opens up before our eyes: a jagged vista of rock spires jutting up from the thickly wooded valley floor. Now, through the trees on our side, we spy the first drop off of this gorge that, over thousands of years, has been etched deep into the porous limestone rocks by the Erlauf River.

We make our way with caution down the steepening narrow path, crossing wooden bridges over summer-soft cascades. The white-red-white horizontal striped trail marker painted at intervals on the rocks tells us we're on the right path—though there's no other alternative now. Our trail threads right along the rock face.

Sheer limestone walls tower above us as we descend through the crevasse, our path becoming a series of wooden-planked bridges riveted into the rock. We cross an avalanche ravine and, looking back, suddenly catch a glimpse of the Lassing Waterfall as it plunges down the vertical walls and into a deep, clear pool far below us. The updraft from the cascade cools us as we continue downwards.

Now it is so steep that we have to go right through the rock! Four tunnels have been cut, one of them like a Gothic arch but the other three so low and Romanesque-rounded that we have to bend down to go through them. To our right, the wall drops straight down to the floor of the gorge below.

We continue our descent towards the streaming river gurgling with foam from that sheer drop-off at the falls. Finally we arrive at the bottom and follow the stream where black monarch butterflies flit around between the wildflowers. After skirting a small hydroelectric power station nestled incongruously in the midst of this otherwise pristine nature, there is even more water and we start ascending now, criss-crossing this rushing stream on bridges seven or eight times over the next hour.

Now we're out in the open on a narrow sandy-sloped path above the stream—and is it ever hot, even for autumn! Rounding a bend, we see that we're not the only ones who think so: here a whole Austrian family has stripped down to bathing suits and is leaping, one after the other, from a boulder into the crystal clear pool below it, laughing and climbing up to do it all over again. Unable to resist the temptation, I make my way down the scree slope with the help of rocks and tree branches, take off my shoes, roll up my pants and—aahh! is that water ever wonderful!

Refreshed, I scramble up the slope and we head for the little outdoor snack shack called the "Ötscher-Hias" for a tall, chilled "G'spritzter" half white-wine, half mineral water. We've been underway just a little over two hours and have one more to go.

Now we leave the floor of the gorge behind and ascend a steep path through the woods that, at the top, feeds into a large dirt road to a picturesque farmhouse that has been converted into an "Urlaub am Bauernhof" hideaway: the "farm vacation" so popular with Austrian families whose children are raised in urban settings. This one is really idyllic with window boxes full of flowers and fields full of cows and ripening corn. Famished, we go in for a meal, a classic Wiener Schnitzel.

Wiener Schnitzel (Breaded Veal Cutlets) and Potato Salad

Any discriminating gourmet knows that the 'Viennese' Schnitzel is, in fact, Milanese (I didn't)! It is said that Field Marshal Radetzky—the one who inspired the famous Radetzky March—brought a recipe for "costoletta milanese" back from Italy in 1848 so that today worldwide acclaim is accorded to the Austrians for having 'invented' it!

Ingredients:

4 veal cutlets (6-7 oz each)	*2 eggs, beaten*	*2 T cream*
Salt, white pepper	*1 cup 8 oz) oil*	*4 T flour*
4 oz bread crumbs	*softened butter*	*Lemon slices parsley*

Rinse the veal cutlets under cold water and pat them dry with a paper towel. Remove any fatty edges to prevent curling. Pound the cutlets on both sides with a cleaver. In a shallow bowl or pie pan, mix the eggs, cream, salt and pepper. Spread the bread crumbs on the bottom of the pie pan.

Heat oil in a large skillet. Put the flour on a plate, add salt and pepper and dredge both sides of the cutlets. Then dip them into the egg mixture and coat them with bread crumbs.

One after the other, place breaded cutlets in hot oil over medium heat and fry for 3-5 min., turning occasionally. While cooking, carefully rotate the pan to ensure that the oil reaches all parts of the cutlets. When both sides are golden brown, remove the cutlets from the oil and drain on absorbent paper towels. Brush with melted butter and serve with lemon wedges and garnished with parsley.

Tyrolean Potato Salad Ingredients:

16 oz salad potatoes	*2 oz smoked, sliced bacon*	*1 medium onion*	
2 T oil		*1 ½ T wine vinegar*	*1 tsp German mustard*
½ cup (4 oz) beef stock	*salt, black pepper, pinch of sugar*	*1 tsp drained capers*	
1 T chives, finely chopped	*Optional: mix in sliced tomatoes, cucumber, cress, lettuce hearts*		

Boil salad potatoes until tender. Drain and let cool to manageable temperature. While still warm, peel and slice them into a large bowl. Finely dice the smoked bacon together with peeled onion. Fry the bacon and onion in oil at medium heat until translucent, stirring constantly. Add vinegar to hot pan and stir. Pour the mixture over the potatoes.

Warm broth, stir in mustard and add to potatoes. Add optional vegetables if desired. Season strongly with salt and pepper and mix well. Serve garnished with fresh, chopped chives as an ideal accompaniment to either Wiener Schnitzel, Fried Chicken and/or Fried Carp.

Note: The Viennese version of this salad omits the bacon and uses a special local potato called the 'Kipfler' that is small, yellow and almost waxy in consistency.

After lunch we stroll leisurely to the "Mariazellerbahn," a old-fashioned, small-gauge private railway that operates only from May through

October. Surrounded by flowers, the station sits all alone in a wooded clearing, like something out of a fairytale. Climbing aboard, we are treated to a scenic ride with yet more panoramas of this wooded "Grand Canyon of Austria" before emerging as from an enchanting dream back where we started.

It only took four hours all-told—but we've had a mini-magic journey to another world!

Before we head home, we make a short detour to the nearby pristine Erlaufsee and take an hour-long stroll around it. The Hapsburg former hunting lodge on the lake shore has been transformed into a restaurant where we enjoy a mélange before setting off for home.

In a Nutshell: Route: Hike in, ride out: hike from Wienerbruck through the Ötschergräben and past the Lassing waterfall to the Erlauf Klause. Hiking time: about 3 hours. Distance: 7 km. Degree of difficulty: medium, surefootedness and no fear of heights is a must. Special features: pre-alpine flora and fauna and „alpine islands" at an altitude of only 600-700 m. Take the Mariazeller train back through one of its most beautiful stretches. Best seasons: May until the end of October. Rest stops: Snack station „Ötscherhias", open May-October.

WINTER IN THE CITY
DECEMBER: Christmas And "Silvester" In Austria

Making Christmas Real: An Austrian Celebration in the Spirit of St. Francis

Austria is a predominantly Christian country with a long Catholic legacy dating back to the times of the Holy Roman Empire. Moreover, it is a country where people habitually greet each other, not with a disinterested "How ya doin?" but with a warm-hearted *"Grüss Gott"*— "God be with you".

Five days during this period are celebrated as national religious holidays: the Feast of the Immaculate Conception (December 8), Christmas (December 25), St. Stephen's Day (December 26), New Year's Day (January 1) and Epiphany (January 6). To emphasize the sacred and family aspects of these days, all offices, stores and even many restaurants are closed.

If Austrians tend to keep their good cheer and composure in the hectic Christmas weeks, it's because they keep the meaning in mind. Unlike many Western countries, Christmas here is not just another excuse for shopping. Instead, the entire six-week period beginning with November's First Sunday in Advent to January's Epiphany is celebrated fully.

Advent Anticipation. A spirit of anticipation permeates Austrian during Advent, the four week period leading up to the central holiday of December 25 that marks the birth of Jesus.

Outdoor Advent markets, first held in Vienna in the 13th century, now thrive throughout the country. Also called "Christkindl Markets", the string of open-air wooden stalls is at its festive best after dark, the snowy market streets illuminated with bright lights and enlivened by wide-eyed children often being carried on their fathers' shoulders to give them a better view of their favourite stalls filled with toys and dolls, balloons and candy.

These decorated outdoor stalls display an astonishing diversity of goods, ranging from hand-carved and blown-glass Christmas tree ornaments to handmade candles and jewelry. And, of course, food and drink! People indulge in steaming cups of hot, mulled wine and down links of hot sausages, roasted chestnuts, giant pretzels, potato pancakes, popcorn and fresh or candied fruit.

Every year, the City of Vienna hosts the most sumptuous (and telegenic) of all Christkindlmärkte right in front of its towering, illuminated neo-Gothic Vienna Town Hall. There, 140 stalls offer an endless variety of festive sights, sounds and smells. Part of the market especially devoted to children features storytelling, pony rides, magic shows and a merry-go-round. Children also participate in activities such as making presents or baking cookies.

Symbols and Celebrations. Assisi may be in Italy but the spirit of St Francis and the humanization of the message of hope and generosity is readily evident in Austria, even down to the trappings. Throughout Austria today, beautiful nativity scenes, such as the crèches created by

St Francis in the 13th century, with live animals and people to bring the Christmas story to life, are displayed in homes, churches, museums and town halls alongside the now ubiquitous Christmas tree. Early Franciscans also wrote carols and spread Christmas music to Austria, where musical celebrations of the season continue to flourish.

> *St. Francis, who enjoyed celebrating the incarnation, would have loved the extended Christmas as it is celebrated in Austria.*

An earlier article on Christmas in Austria refers to a visit to the ancient Franciscan friary in the heart of Vienna—St. Hieronymus (St. Jerome) Church, a 1603 Renaissance building with the city's oldest organ. Despite the flamboyant 18th-century baroque high altar that rises dramatically all the way to the ceiling, the Franciscans keep their feet on the ground and serve especially the poor in practical ways. One way is providing a simple breakfast for about 60 poor people at the friary each morning. Another is the special Christmas dinner typically served to 100-200 people each year on 26 December to mark the Feast of St. Stephen. St Jerome Church displays a copy of a painting by the famous Austrian artist Ferdinand Waldmüller (1793-1865) of friars feeding needy people at this same house more than 150 years ago. The priest says, "Franciscans have always been popular in Austria because they work with and are close to the people. Our annual Stephanitag dinner for the poor keeps us in touch with our traditions."

So Austrian Christmas is still "robustly religious" and that is how it can be best appreciated. To help visitors understand and celebrate this season along with the Austrians, the Vienna city tourist information offices distribute a free and comprehensive brochure in English, entitled *Advent and Christmas in Vienna: Events and Information.* Published by the Archdiocese of Vienna, the brochure lists Masses and other services (including the music to be performed) for all Catholic and other Christian churches.

Historical and biblical background is given not only for major feasts but also for a fascinating array of minor feasts such as *St. Nicholas Day on December 6.* On that day in Austria, people dressed as the saint are often accompanied by a wicked furry devil called Krampus, who gives coal or sticks to bad children. The original St. Nicholas was a fourth-century bishop in Asia Minor. His feast day is loved by Austrian children, who receive small gifts of sweets and toys.

Music: A Sacred Tradition. In Austria—and especially in Salzburg—music is everywhere, not only in the churches. Now "the night before Christmas" is nearing as we enjoy a mug of steaming hot punch outside on the Cathedral Square (Domplatz). We watch as a children's choir sings Christmas carols and presents a small play on the cathedral steps. No sooner do they finish than a brass band tunes up and begins to play in a nearby courtyard. Snow begins to fall but, with such a lively scene, it is no surprise that we and hundreds of others brave the freezing weather to shop, eat, drink and socialize until nine or ten at night.

On Christmas Eve Day we visit Salzburg's city museum to see a crèche collection, two dozen or so antique and contemporary nativity scenes. In one crèche, the Holy Family was serenaded by dozens of figures representing characters from well-known operas such as Mozart's *The Magic Flute.* As we emerge at noon, the stores and most restaurants are closing for Christmas Eve and Day, as well as the feast of St. Stephen. Even our hotel restaurant will be closed for the next three days. The desk clerk apologizes, "In Austria, people want to celebrate Christmas with their families."

So that afternoon, we take a short trip through forests of snow-covered evergeens to the town of **Oberndorf** where, a special Christmas Eve ceremony commemorates the first ever performance of "Silent Night" in 1818. The carol was composed by Franz Xavier Gruber, the parish organist, for lyrics written by Father Joseph Mohr, the assistant pastor. The song was first played at Midnight Mass on Father Mohr's guitar, because the organ was not working. A simple white chapel with stained-glass windows built in the 1930s commemorates the original church, which was destroyed in a flood. A beautiful program of Christmas music by the town choir and brass band ended with a moving rendition of the song.

We return to attend the ten o'clock Christmas Mass at Salzburg's Franciscan church, part of the building complex housing the residence of the prince-archbishops who ruled the city for hundreds of years until 1805. We arrive just on time as the doors are opening at 9:30 p.m., but the large crowd ahead of us means that we are lucky to get the very last seats. Cloaked in darkness, the church's stark Gothic outlines are barely visible, but at ten o'clock sharp, with the playing of "Silent Night", the altar suddenly explodes into light. The music for the remainder of the two-hour service is Gruber's *Mass in D Sharp*, supplemented by several versions of his famous carol.

Christmas morning we go to the main cathedral for the two-hour celebration of Christmas Day Mass with wonderful music. The temperature inside these unheated churches is frigid just like it is outside (ca. 0° Celsius). Thermal underwear and layers of clothing including gloves are essential. Despite these difficult conditions, both Masses include full complements of soloists, choir and orchestra.

For the remainder of Christmas, Salzburg offers more than a dozen additional musical events. We choose a harp concert in the cozy lounge of a hotel in Monchstein Castle, 1,000 feet above the town. An hour of gentle harp solos conclude with "Silent Night"—an appropriate end to a perfect Austrian Christmas celebration of music outdoors, in churches and finally in a warm room!

How Silvester Got Its Name. Arriving next day in Vienna, we return to visit the Franciscans at St. Jerome's and learn that their annual December 26 celebration was a success with over 150 poor people served a meal of Wiener schnitzel and salad, supplemented by Gospel readings, in a large room at the friary.

Emphasizing that the spirit of Christmas is enjoyed throughout the season, Father Gottfried tells us that in Austria, New Year's celebrations are named for the December 31 feast day of fourth-century Pope Sylvester I. Vienna is justly famous for its "Silvester" operettas, balls and concerts. But there is also an impressive range of **religious events** throughout town. St. Augustine Church at the Hapsburg Palace holds Sylvester celebrations at 5 p.m. (Mozart's *Coronation Mass*) and the next day at 11 a.m. (Schubert's *Mass in B Sharp*).

As we leave the friary, Father Gottfried shows us an inscription chalked over several hallway doors—"C+M+B" with the year, explaining that this annual Epiphany inscription serves as a reminder of its two meanings—the blessing *"Christus mansionem benedicat"* (May Christ bless this house) as well as the initials of the Three Kings (Casper, Melchior and Balthazar).

And, lo and behold, as we emerge from the friary, we see the Three Kings themselves! Carrying a replica of the star of Bethlehem, three young girls dressed in the bright robes of the Magi are singing Christmas and Epiphany carols. "Star singers" such as these visit homes and cafes, hospitals and senior citizen centres to chalk over the door the same blessing we just saw within the friary.

We conclude our Christmas Season with the conviction that St Francis himself—who so enjoyed celebrating the incarnation that makes Christmas real—would have loved the extended Season as it is celebrated here in Austria.

Fiaker Goulash

The year 1693 marked the licensing of what remains to this day a colourful Viennese tradition: the official hackney—or 'Fiaker'—coachman. These authentic drivers still don their traditional costumes—houndstooth trousers, velvet jacket and top hat—to ply the inner district's narrow cobblestone lanes with their pairs of romantic, horse-drawn carriages. Just as unique—and spicy—is the Hungarian-based 'Gulyas' that warmed them on cold winter nights. By the way, this is one of the dishes that get better with time so, by all means, serve it as a 'leftover'!

Ingredients:

2 lbs of beef for roasting	1 ½ lbs onions	2 T oil or shortening
2 T sweet paprika powder	1 T vinegar	3 cups (24 oz) beef stock
2 crushed garlic cloves	pinch of marjoram	½ tsp ground caraway
1 T tomato paste	4 eggs	4 frankfurters
Salt, pepper	4 pickles (garnish)	

Rinse the beef under cold water, pat dry with a paper towel and cut into large cubes. Peel the onions and chop them finely. Pour oil into a large skillet and sauté onions until golden brown. Sprinkle with sweet paprika powder. Add vinegar and several tablespoons of beef stock.

Now add the cubed meat and spices. Reduce the heat, cover and simmer for about 1 ½ hours, stirring frequently and adding beef stock as required. When the meat is tender, add the remaining beef stock, tomato paste and crushed garlic. Simmer for 10 more minutes and season to taste.

Spoon goulash into soup bowls and garnish with a fried egg, frankfurter and a gherkin cut in fan form. **Bon apétit!**

Styrian Wine Soup & Schilcher Rosé

Ingredients:

3-5 slices dried white rolls	*2-3 T butter*	*1 tsp ground cinnamon*
4 cups (1 ¾ pt) white wine	*4-5 T sugar*	*grated rind of 1 lemon*
6-8 egg yolks, beaten	*4 T sour cream*	

Cut rolls into cubes, brown in butter and sprinkle with cinnamon. Put aside.

Bring white wine to a boil, add sugar and grated lemon rind. Reduce heat. Combine egg yolks and cream. Beat slowly into wine with a wire whisk. Serve soup topped with cinnamon croutons.

JANUARY: Vienna's Ball Season—& Some You've Never Seen!

THE SACHER PRELUDE

Outrageously handsome, I catch myself thinking, taking his arm as we exit Vienna's famed Hotel Sacher just across the street from the even more renowned *Staatsoper* (State Opera).

My escort, Helmut, is Austria incarnate with his lilting, Viennese-accented English, his trachten coat and dapper felt hat, his slim, sporty physique and his friendly-flirtatious smile. *Irresistibly charming* in the inimitable way that Austrians have cultivated over the centuries. This trait is what helped the Hapsburg Empire to expand into a 17th century realm "upon which the sun never set" and substituted marriages for the ravages of war, leading to the Latin epithet:

> *Bella gerant alii, tu, felix Austria, nube.*
> *Nam quae Mars aliis, dat tibi regna Venus*

> Let the strong fight wars. Thou, happy Austria, wed.
> What Mars bestows on others, Venus gives to thee instead.[1]

Though today 'happy Austria's' globe-spanning Empire is but a memory, the charm is as delectable as ever. Helmut is living proof.

This evening's intimate dinner in the fabled red-velvet-and-candlelight Sacher Restaurant was *his* invitation—ostensibly business—but how could anyone talk business in such a seductive setting, complete with a Lizst-like pianist playing the *Barcarole* from *Hoffman's Tales*?

The dinner features the Sacher's specialities—melt-in-your-mouth *Tafelspitz* with apple horseradish, creamed spinach and Rösti topped off by a superbly chilled Gruener Veltiner and followed by the chocolate 'Torte' that gave the Sacher its name. This is Austria *par excellence*. Including the company.

---

1   *The Marrying of Anne of Cleves: Royal Protocol in Early Modern England, Retha M. Warnicke, Cambridge University Press, 2000, p. 5. This epithet, that captures the essence of the method the Habsburgs used to expand their presence in Europe, was coined in 1477 by King Matthias Corvinus of Hungary, who actually intended to mock their military incompetence, not to celebrate their marital strategies. It stands, however, as an accurate description of how they achieved their dynastic advantages in the bedchamber.*

Tafelspitz—Boiled Beef—with Apple Horseradish

Ingredients:

2 lbs of beef bones	*4 ½ lbs loin of beef or brisket*	*1 small parsley root, chopped*
1-2 carrots, chopped	*2 celery sticks, chopped*	*1 small leek*
2 garlic cloves, crushed	*2 small onions*	*1 bay leaf*
3 T chives, finely chopped	*Pinch of nutmeg*	*Salt*

Sauce:

2 medium apples	*2 T wine vinegar*	*2-3 T grated horseradish*
1-2 tsp sugar	*pinch of salt*	*white pepper to taste*

Rinse the beef soup bones and place them in a large pot. Cover them with water, add salt and bring to a boil. Add beef. Bring to a boil once again and skim the liquid several times if necessary. Reduce the heat.

But, before we go on, let's stop for a delicious bit of history about the Hotel Sacher and its Torte, as related by Elizabeth Gürtler, reigning fourth generation queen of Vienna's famed Sacher family. As she tells it:

"The story of the Sacher all started with a cake! The year was 1832 and the place was the Viennese court of Prince Metternich, Austria's Minister of Foreign Affairs and a personality who dominated European politics for the first half of the 19th century.

In keeping with the elegance of the 1813-1815 Congress of Vienna, another of the court's glittering soirées was to be held—but someone had forgotten to notify the head chef who had left on holiday! What was to be done?!

Sixteen-year-old apprentice cook Franz Sacher to the rescue! In those days before fridges, one of young Franz's main challenges was to come up with a dessert that could be prepared in advance but not go bad. Also being an epoch of culinary indulgence pre-dating diets by two centuries, he proceeded to concoct a "light dessert" containing eight (!) egg yolks and apricot jam and conserved by a thick, rich glaze of dark chocolate and sugar. A sinner's delight, the torte that took his name became all the rage, and its hand-written recipe later a "state secret" of the Hotel Sacher that was subsequently opened on its present site in 1868.

Franz's son, Edward ran the original hotel, called "Hotel de l'Opéra, located as it is vis-à-vis the Vienna State Opera House. But the name was changed to "Hotel Sacher" after Edward married the much younger Anna, a butcher's daughter who became one of Vienna's most colourful personalities. A friend of the arts scene, Anna was something of an actress herself, smoking cigars, sporting a shoulder tattoo and collecting Chihuahua dogs as a hobby.

Just as it was Anna's boldness and business acumen that put the Sacher on the map, it was also Anna who created the exclusive "chambers séparées" for the "enfants terribles" of Vienna's Gilded Age, protecting them when necessary from exposure and police raids. Although the Emperor boycotted the Sacher, that didn't stop it from becoming famous, if not notorious. In fact, there is a story that circulates to this day that Emperor Karl's son, Otto, one of the more debauched of the Hapsburg clan, once descended the red-carpeted staircase after a night of revelry, clad only in his Imperial belt and saber. The British Ambassador's wife, who had come to pay her respects, promptly fainted. Such were the days—and nights—at the Sacher.

But all good things must come to an end and so, when Anna passed away in 1930 at the age of 75, the Sacher entered a more sedate, then somber period, accumulating debts and drifting under the ominous cloud of insolvency.

However, it survived and today has re-emerged, thriving, as Austria's only privately owned five-star hotel. It retains a uniquely Viennese patina in terms of its atmosphere, interior décor, extensive private collection of artwork, and family presence. Not only that. In order to compete successfully with the likes of big hotel chains like the Sheraton and Intercontinental, it has just expanded, adding 45 new rooms on a new top floor, as well as a Sacher Spa with—what else?—special chocolate treatments that release those yummy endorphins."

So now, would you like to know about the torte after which a hotel dynasty is named?

Sachertorte

The recipe below is a close approximation of the original, and still heavily guarded, secret of the Sacher Hotel dynasty, whose famed hotel reigns vis-à-vis the Vienna State Opera.

Ingredients:

5 oz butter	*4 oz sifted powdered sugar*	*8 egg yolks*
5 oz dark chocolate	*5 oz (2/3 cup) flour*	*8 egg whites*
2 oz sugar	*2 T apricot jam*	*8 oz (1 cup) cream*
	4 oz dark chocolate glaze	

Cream the softened butter and powdered sugar. Beat in egg yolks one after another until the mixture is thick and creamy.

Melt bittersweet chocolate in a double boiler or microwave, stir until lukewarm, then stir into cream by the teaspoonful. Sift in flour. Beat egg whites with sugar until stiff. Gently fold into chocolate mixture with a wire whisk.

Line the bottom of a 9-inch spring form pan with a baking paper circle. Spread batter evenly and bake in a 340-375 degree F oven for 50-55 minutes. Remove and let cool for several minutes. Then run a knife around the cake and remove the sides of the pan. Let the cake cool completely on a wire rack. Remove paper and, if necessary, even out the cake bottom with a knife.

Stir and warm apricot preserves. Smooth over entire cake, including the sides. Melt commercial chocolate glaze to frost cake. Decorate as desired, slice with a moistened, serrated knife and serve with unsweetened whipped cream and original Sacher coffee.

And while you're indulging your sweet tooth, know that you are not alone! Each year, the Sacher uses 2.8 million eggs and produces 350,000 tortes to be devoured by people just like us all over the world!

Back to the Sacher Restaurant and my Austrian dinner partner. The workaday world forgotten, we bask in the elegant ambiance and each other's presence. Talk turns to skiing deep powder at Heiligenblut in the shadow of the Grossglockner, Austria's highest summit (which we have both climbed, though not together). He waxes eloquent about the glories of skiing off-piste and by the time we leave, I have promised myself to follow suit.

Outside it's February frigid for the first time this winter. As we walk arm in arm up the pedestrian Kaerntnerstrasse towards St. Stephan's Cathedral in the heart of the city, lights twinkle in sophisticated shop windows, the wind whispers of coming snow, and people in the streets are bundled up but cheery.

"Helmut, I'd like to have *you* in my book about Austria," I say on the spur of the moment. "What could we do together that's traditionally Austrian—but off the beaten track? Where could we go exploring some back country to find some forgotten treasures?"

"That's easy," he counters, "Krems! And then a bike tour of the Wachau when the apricot and cherry trees bloom!"

WALTZING VIENNA: "Alles Waltzer!"

Opera Ball: Waltzes in White Organza "Vergangenheit"

"Alles Waltzer!" "Everyone, waltz!" This is the magical exhortation that sets Austria awhirl in three-quarter tact each winter! Vienna's Ball Season is perhaps the world's most resplendent with more than 300 events crowded into a short January-February social calendar.

There are balls for all backgrounds, tastes and pocketbooks: everything from the world renowned Opera Ball that has been held in Vienna's elegant Opera House since 1877 to the Emperor's Ball in the Hofburg that rings in the New Year to the Philharmonic Ball held in the Musikverein where the New Year's Day concert is broadcast throughout the world each year.

But there is also an astonishing array of other balls—the Masked Ball, the Doctors' Ball, the Hunters' Ball, the Lawyers' Ball, the Psychotherapists'

Ball, the Firemen's Ball, the Coffeebrewers' Ball, the Pastrymakers' Ball, the Veterinarians' Ball, even a Refugees' Ball! No one is left out in this tradition that is actually rooted in Austria's Catholic past.

What does devout Catholicism have to do with dancing? you may ask. The answer is "a lot." As a predominantly Catholic country, many of Austria's traditions—like this mid-winter carnival season—are linked to the Christian calendar, in this case the festive period that precedes Lent. The ball scene acquired an unmatched sheen of elegance during the 600-year period when the Hapsburgs reigned from Vienna's Hofburg. Even today balls staged at the Hofburg cast a spell over their guests, making them suspect they have slipped through a time warp into an earlier century.

So it is for this frosty February night, standing on the red carpeted steps of the Hofburg foyer, all aglow with gold, glitter and glamourous couples in full evening dress, making their way up to the Festival Hall for the opening ceremonies. The only thing that would tip one off that we're not back in the days of the 1813-1815 Congress of Vienna is the host of this particular ball—which is the International Atomic Energy Agency staff association.

IAEA Ball: The "nuclear watchdog" waltzes!

Yes, 'the Agency' has its own ball, too! And a magnificent one at that, this year boasting some 3,000 guests! Quite a far cry, this, from the usual pubic image of head-to-toe white-clad inspectors in one of Bush's 'axis of evil' countries searching for weapons of mass destruction. Along with its work in the area of peaceful nuclear applications, this is another of the Agency's less known faces.

Now, the Master of Ceremonies introduces one of the Agency's Deputy Directors General, who observes that, 'while Europe is only *speaking* about it, America is actually *making* world history.'—referring in part to the Nobel Peace Prize that the Agency and its Director General Mohamed ElBaradei were awarded in 2006. The IAEA, too, is 'working to make its mark on both the Viennese *and* world history,' he concludes, leaving us to reflect on America's current power politics against the backdrop of Austria's European hegemony just a few centuries ago.

Much as they seem eternal at their apogee, empires are transient things … just as this evening is. We turn our attention back to the moment and its festivities. The parkett is cleared for an entourage of Viennese couples, the young men in formal black evening dress, the flushed young ladies all in white with delicate pink rose corsages at their wrists. Now they open the ball with deep curtsies followed by the most elegant of waltzes, sweeping sixty strong around the main 'Festsaal' to the strains of the Emperor's Waltz, their gowns and graceful movements illuminated by rows of sparkling chandeliers overhead and captured in meter high mirrors around the room.

If I didn't know better, I might even suspect that the spirits of Emperor Franz Josef and his beloved Elisabeth were right here in our midst! http://www.aboutaustria.org/veranstaltungen/ *****

LIFE BALL: A Lifestyle Extravaganza

Life Ball, the biggest Charity Event to fight HIV and AIDS in Europe, is an annual ball taking place in Vienna. Under the motto of solidarity and tolerance, the Life Ball celebrates life and unifies people of all social classes with the aim to raise money for the persons affected, but also to give information about this disease and its prevention.

This year the Life Ball is taking place on May 26, 2007 and is on that occasion also celebrating its 15th jubilee. The organiser of the Life Ball, Aids Life, was founded in 1992 as a charitable society with the aim to provide selected non-profit organisations, which directly support HIV-positive persons and persons infected with AIDS, with as much financial means as possible. Besides this, Aids Life moves this topic, which seems to always fall behind, in the centre of the public attention, thus giving the affected persons a voice.

One half of the net proceeds – in 2006 the Life Ball managed to obtain 1,111,000 Euro only in one night - are donated to the national programs, whereas the other half is allocated in cooperation with internationally renowned organisations, such as the American Foundation for Aids Research (amfAR), to the areas of the world most affected with HIV and AIDS.

The opening ceremony of the ball, consisting of a spectrum of artistic program scenes and the traditional fashion show of a world famous designer, is taking place at the Viennese Rathausplatz (City Hall Square) and is freely accessible to some 40,000 visitors. Afterwards, 4,000 people possessing the Life Ball ticket may enter the Rathaus (City Hall), where in all halls and courts of the building they can enjoy the live acts of international stars, exciting performances, dancefloors and rich offer in gastronomy.

With their performances and personal engagement the participating artists set an important sign for life and against prejudices. Thus, they render an enormous contribution for the success of the Life Ball.

More information on the programme and proceeds of the Life Ball is regularly updated on the official Life Ball website: www.lifeball.org

---

Heatherette stages the Life Ball Show in 2007

The hip US Designer Duo Richie Rich and Traver Rains—alias Heatherette—bring exalted glamour and cool New York chic to the Life Ball 2007 catwalk in front of the Viennese City Hall.

„We are very proud and extremely excited to bring the world of Heatherette to Life Ball 2007!! Being the first designers outside of Europe to take part in this magical event, makes this venture to Vienna a monumental one for us," say Richie Rich and Traver Rains.

In 1999 Heatherette opened with a collection of T-shirts and leather goods and started their unusual story of success. The whole New York fashion scene quickly became interested in their creations: Beginning with the famous stylist Patricia Field who asked them to do the "Carrie"-T-Shirt for "Sex and the City", and David LaChapelle who produces fashion-editorials, to numerous celebrities from the film and music industry who proudly wear their creations.

Since their beginnings at New York Gay Night Clubs, Heatherette have delighted audiences with their incomparable mix of punk-glamour and good humor, and have become major trend setters in The Big Apple – much the same as their musical counterparts The Scissor Sisters.

Richie Rich and Traver Rains have also launched Heatherette internationally, and secured a long list of top celebrities worldwide on board. Today stars such as Gwen Stefani, Paris Hilton, Mariah Carey, Christina Aguilera, Kelly Osbourne, Mary J. Blige, Lil' Kim, David Beckham, Shakira, Courtney Love, Naomi Campbell, Alicia Keys, Pink, Missy Elliott, Pamela Anderson, Beyoncé, Jessica Simpson and The Scissor Sisters belong to the Heatherette-Universe.

With Heatherette, the Life Ball is exactly at the pulse of time and shows for its 15th anniversary the most authentic Life Ball fashion show in its history. "Heatherette are most likely at the moment the wildest and funkiest designer duo in the world and they fit the Life Ball non-conformist and life-affirmative spirit absolutely perfectly," explains Life Ball Organizer Gery Keszler.

„We see the opportunity to take part in such a powerful event as an opportunity of a lifetime, and promise to deliver a fashion show with heart, conviction and a lot of sparkle! So get ready to take a ride over the rainbow and experience the Heatherette fairytale… a dream of love and compassion," emphasize Richie Rich and Traver Rains and look forward to the Life Ball Fashion Show 2007.

For further information on current Life Ball activities, please contact Life Ball Press, Claudia Greif, Tel. +43 1 595 40 26 or presse@lifeball. org

www.lifeball.org, www.stylebible.org

FEBRUARY: Carneval In Bad Aussee

Styrian "Fasching, Flinserl and Trommelweiber"

Picture-postcard Austria. I can't help it if that sounds trite—that's just the way it looks! Sparkling expanses of white beneath a dome of deep blue unblemished by a single cloud. The pristine peaks of the Loser, Trisselwand and the more distant Dachstein massif surround us with the almost theatrical winter wonderland of Bad Aussee in the Styrian Salzkammergut.

Of course, there's a price to pay for all this splendor: the heavy snowfalls of the past three days have caused the closing of the train route due to acute avalanche danger, meaning that, instead of the usual direct train link from Vienna, we now have to disembark near Bad Goisern and clamber by bus over the Pötschen Pass that connects the province of Salzburg to that of Styria.

Still, the driver sighs with relief, saying that a squadron of some 15 snowploughs has been working through the night to clear the roads. We see the evidence in house-high snow banks and say a silent thanks that we are arriving today rather than three days ago. It's February and time for 'Fasching', otherwise known as *Mardi Gras or Carneval* , the period just preceding Lent.

The Blaue Traube (Blue Grape) is a traditional old gasthof in Bad Aussee, a village geographically at the center of Austria dating back to Roman times and with an original engraved gravestone in the gasthof's entrance hall to prove it! My friend Laura and I are shown to our room, which amazes us with its luxurious size, view and massive, highly polished antique furniture—no pre-fab, olive-drab, all-of-a-kind Holiday Inn, this! But, impressive as it is, we're not here just for a 'room with a view'.

So we grab our cross-country skis and head straight for the Sun Loop and Summer Mountain Lake Loop that feed into the spectacular 8-km long Dachstein Panorama Loop. The track is perfectly prepared, two parallel sets of grooves winding like a silver ribbon through the alpine snowscape. Herring-boning up, slip-sliding down the gentle fir-studded hills, time disappears as tiny hamlets arise and descend in slow motion, now on our right, now on our left, into the contoured snow. Like one of those 3-D children's picture books. Magnificent silence. Not a soul this late afternoon to mar the mood or break the spell of sheer perfection. Haiku poems form like crystals in my mind:

> *shhh…shhh…shhh…shhh—sounds*
> *of skate-skiers on the track*
> *I breathe in the sun*

*****

154

white sun warms my face
blue snow fills the shadows
cold breath sparkles silver

By the time we glide back through the blueing hills and into a mauve, post-sunset sky, my legs signal 'enough' for the first day. But Laura, a ten-year resident of Anchorage who regularly skied Kincaid Park's night-lit track, is unfazed by this 'short' 15.5 km run.

Back at the Blaue Traube, we take our cue from the name of the place and stop for a Glühwein—hot red wine spiced with cloves and cinnamon—before heading up to shower. At dinner we share a convivial table and a delicious dinner washed down with Austrian wine, followed by delicious traditional desserts—Apfelstrudel and Kaiserschmarrn (See Vignette #2 for the latter)—to restore whatever calories we may have shed through our cross-country exertions.

❖   APFELSTRUDEL à la Sacher

Ingredients:

Strudel pastry (self- or ready-made). If self-made pastry, prepare as follows.

250 g fine flour	2 egg yolks for daubing
Pinch of salt	icing sugar for dusting
1 Tbsp oil	Oil
2 Tbsps melted butter for daubing	Flour for the work surface
125 ml lukewarm water	Butter for daubing

Preparation

For the pastry, heap some flour onto a work surface and knead the pastry ingredients into a smooth, elastic dough. Shape into a ball and place in a soup bowl dribbled with oil. Cover and refrigerate, preferably over night. Next day, on a lightly floured surface, roll out the pastry dough into a square with a rolling pin. Pull until very thin. To do this, make sure your hands are covered in flour, place one hand under the dough and use the other hands to carefully pull the dough out from the center. The dough should become so thin that it is almost transparent.

Add remaining ingredients to the:

Strudel pastry (self- or ready-made)

1.5 kg Elstar (or similar) apples

Juice from 1 lemon

60 g raisins soaked in rum

200 g melted butter

100 g sugar

2 Tbsps vanilla sugar

100 g breadcrumbs

pinch of cinnamon powder

Butter for daubing

Icing sugar for dusting

1 egg for daubing

Preparation

Peel and seed the apples. Slice very thin. Dribble with lemon juice to prevent discolouration. In a separate bowl, combine 2 T of raisins and 1 T vanilla sugar. Brush the pastry dough with half the melted butter, using the rest to fry the breadcrumbs. Combine crumbs with the rest of the vanilla sugar and cinnamon and sprinkle over the pastry. Distribute the apple slices evenly over the pastry. Roll with the help of a dish towel. Make sure the ends are well closed. Place the strudel on a greased baking tray (for a small tray, bend it into a horseshoe shape). Brush with the beaten egg and bake in a preheated over at 180ºC for 30-40 minutes, occasionally brushing with melted butter. When done, let the strudel cool and dust with icing sugar. Strudel can be served either warm or cold.

Guten appetit!

Laura's in high form, too, regaling our table of six with stories of her globe-trotting adventures before joining the Vienna-based OPEC Secretariat as an energy analyst.

"Oh, nothing much fazes me," says she, *"I was one of a handful of female chemical engineers at Tulane and then decided to specialize in oil and gas extraction, carbon sequestration, you know."* We *don't*—until she explains that this is a technique to capture carbon molecules and thus reduce greenhouse gas emissions. *"Well, and then during the ten years I spent on Alaska's North Slope …"* and off she goes on another tale of her adventures in the far north, contrasted with postings to the Persian Gulf and South America, before skipping off to do a mid-career MPA at Harvard's Kennedy School. Laura takes us on an exhilarating mental journey around the world before returning us to Austria in time for an after-dinner coffee with whipped cream.

Now we're ready for *Fasching* and the traditional Styrian 'Trachten Ball' that launches a giddy four-day celebration before the onset of Lent. Staged at the elegant 'Kurhaus' in the center of the village, it boasts two bands and animated trachten-clad couples of the 30+ variety dancing waltzes interspersed with minuet-type square dances and, at midnight, a quadrille. Everybody's having a rollicking time, especially the white-bearded elder who takes a turn with every woman at the ball.

Day Two dawns clear and still and we're off bright and early to the Blaa Alm on the Loser Toll Road where there is both alpine and cross-country skiing. We spend the morning stretching our legs on another perfectly-laid track and metaphorically scrubbing our lungs with the fresh, crisp air in between a hearty outdoor lunch of soup and salad at a trailside gasthof.

Then a bunch of us return mid-afternoon to leave ourselves time for Bad Aussee's newly renovated 'Vital Bad' with its spacious, glassed-in thermal pool and array of steam baths, saunas and outdoor courtyards for plunging naked into the snow. Exhilarating but not everyone's favorite pastime.

At dinner, our Hiking Club colleagues come masked-and-costumed, especially our leader Christine who is hilariously camouflaged as a moustached, bespectacled 'Sheikh Ahmed' complete with flowing white robes. Rollicking fun, delicious cheese dumplings (Käsnockerl) and swift-flowing wine: before I know it, the day's escapades do me in; I'm sound asleep by ten.

Day Three dawns charmed and cloudless once again! Good so because today is the day of the 'Trommelweiber.' Going down early for breakfast, we don't know quite what to expect.

"Hey, what's all that stuff on the table? It's full of big bass drums … and look!" Laura points, bursting into high-pitched giggles, *"an unclaimed pair of plastic boobies! Now who do you suppose left those?"*

Our interest piqued, we tiptoe down and crack open the door to the Stube to reveal—a room full of ***men***—the 'Drummer Dames'—decked out like 17th century women in starched-and-corseted, ankle-length nightdresses, lace sleeping caps and, to preserve anonymity, full face masks. This tradition dates back to pagan times when the racket made by masked villagers was meant to exorcise the evil spirits of everything from lightning to hailstorms. It is noteworthy that it's not capricious youngsters but, in fact, some 60 of the town's most respected elders and leaders who perform this ritual.

They begin this day-long gauntlet in our very gasthaus and as one huge hulk of a forester with whom I pose for a photo confides, *"This is no child's play; it's hard work! We go for four days straight, from the Trachten Ball through the Flinseln, and for all of this time have to forego all sources of income and, what's worst, women!"* I remind him that *he* is a woman, at least in costume, but somehow that doesn't seem to placate him.

The last day of Styrian Fasching features yet another spectacle—the 'Flinserl,' more of the masked fantasy of Fasching, this time with Venice-inspired costumes replete with embroidered silver spangles and glitter. The personification of Spring, these masqueraders that remind us of medieval harlequins, parade through the narrow lanes, tossing nuts and oranges from huge bags to the children who recite ritual poems ending with "Nuss! Nuss! Nuss!" to get their booty.

Out in the narrow streets now, the whole town turns out to accompany its Flinserl on their 'rites of spring' until we reach the village's main square where three of us peel off towards Altaussee, a six-km walk, most of it on the snow-packed Elisabeth Promenade, named after 'Sisi,' the much-revered last Empress of Austria.

One o'clock finds us ravenous at the outskirts of Altaussee, a lakeside, summit-encircled village that has been described as 'an alpine Brigadoon', seemingly unchanged for centuries. During the Hapsburg Empire, the salt mined here was so valuable that Altausseers were forbidden to leave, and outsiders forbidden to enter, without a special passport. Luckily, we don't need one.

We hasten down to the Seevilla, a romantic hideaway recalling Altaussee's aristocratic past that was first set in motion back in the 16th century when Archduke Johann, the younger brother of Emperor Franz I, met and fell in love with the postmaster's daughter, Anna Plöchl, who lived in Bad Aussee. Those were the days when marrying a non-royal was unheard of but Johann had his heart set and, after an eleven-year wait, permission for this morganatic marriage was granted, thus "upgrading" Ausseerland and attracting noble families. By the 19th century, this area became a summer Shangri-la for high nobility, landed gentry, upper bourgeoisie and finally *fin de siècle* Viennese intelligentsia. We find ourselves lunching in the Brahms Stube, complete with grand piano and an elegant menu that reminds us that the famous Austrian composer premiered two of his works right here.

As for us, gazing out over the placid expanse of frozen, snow-quilted lake backed by the vertical wall of the Trisselwand where time seems to have stopped altogether, we are suddenly rudely awakened by our watches and have to call a taxi so as not to miss our train back to Vienna.

Still, I am far from satiated by the beauty. I promise myself to return in May for the Narcissus Festival that, I am assured, is "unvergesslich"— unforgettable.

SPRING IN THE COUNTRYSIDE

MARCH: Yoga In Tyrol

Yoga in Tyrol. Counterintuitive? Not really ... though a little explanation helps!

The Himalayas is one of the cradles of Yoga, which originated in India thousands of years ago. It was there, in Rishikesh in the 1950s, that Swami Sivananda (1887-1963) launched the movement now named after him with the exhortation to "serve, love, give, purify, meditate, realize". His Divine Life Society flourished and in 1957 he sent his foremost disciple, Swami Vishnudevananda (1927-1993), to spread the message of yoga to the West. Such was his success that Sivananda is now the largest yoga organization in the world with more than 50 centres in existence, nine of them in Europe.

Considering its Himalayan history, creating an alpine ashram, even in Christian/Catholic Austria is not so surprising. When Swami Vishnudevananda first visited this part of the Tyrol in 1970s, he was electrified, exclaiming, *"Mountains, rivers, lakes, fresh air—it's just like the Himalayas!"* That sense of connection led Sivananda back to Tyrol and the Wilde Kaiser twenty years later.

Thus, the ashram—or "retreat house"—in Reith bei Kitzbühel opened in 1998. Located on an idyllic hilltop, it is overlooked by the magnificent Wilde Kaiser, the "Wild Emperor". The setting is perfect all year 'round and people come from all around the world—from Japan to South Africa to South America to San Francisco, not to forget next-door neighbour Germany, to practice yoga here in this scenic splendor.

As for me, having spent many months in New England's Kripalu Centre for Yoga and Health during my years in the States, I'm thoroughly delighted to discover this centre right just where I would have dreamed it should be! Right next to Kitzbühel with its family ties for me.

My first encounter with Sivananda-Tyrol takes place in the company of Laura and Cheryl, two American friends who are visiting Kitzbühel for the first time. From my past Kitzbühel connections, the town and its environs are familiar to me, but not the yoga center. This is a discovery for all of us!

We arrive on a Friday afternoon in early March after driving from Vienna for our Yoga and Skiing weekend. Passing by the Wilde Kaiser, etched silver into the sky's blue, we reach Reith, take a sharp right turn and head up the snowy hill to the yoga centre housed in several chalets grouped around a central building. Checking into the adjacent Bio-hotel Florian, we store the skis, leave the luggage in our triple room and, after a delicious, light vegetarian supper, head for our first Sivananda session.

Outside, ice crystals float silently through the silver night air and the snow crunches under our boots. Inside all is warmly lit in orange. The mood is mindful, reverent, as we enter the large yet cozy meditation hall, having left our shoes outside. People are seated on pillows scattered about the floor with colourful shawls draped about their shoulders. This is our first experience with Sivananda "Satsang", which is Sanskrit for "in the company of truth". Some sixty people have gathered for two hours of 'Kirtan' chanting, mantra recitations, short classical readings, and meditation on the message.

Sanskrit, we are reminded, is the world's most ancient and holy language with a tonal structure that embodies mystical energies. With the help of printed texts and accompanied by the traditional harmonium, we join in and, indeed, feel the strangeness of the unusual sounds and rhythms. Satsang takes place every morning and evening and, before we go off to bed, it is suggested that we invite its rhythms and wisdom into our dreams. I, for one, sleep very soundly and well until …

"Brringg!" Five o'clock wake-up call. Still half-asleep, we don comfortable yoga clothes and stumble to a practice hall for morning Pranayama, deep breathing exercises that wake us up, followed by meditation, mantra-chanting and a lecture. These exercises, we are told, are most effective when done in the pre-dawn hours between 0400 and 0600 and then again at twilight. Glad I'm a morning person!

The morning session is conducted by Swami Ramapriyananda, a two-decade Sivananda "elder" from Bavaria who heads the Reith Centre. Her lecture, simultaneously translated into two languages (German into English and French), emphasizes the importance of doing yogic practices regularly each day at the same time in the same place. She assures us that 20-60 minutes of such daily meditation, accompanied by deep breathing and concentration of attention either on the "third eye" or in the heart chakra, will calm the mind and harmonize the thoughts. The eventual goal of dedicated yoga practitioners is to pass beyond the state of worldly duality into Samadhi or overarching consciousness. Although this process takes years, if not lifetimes, to refine, there is no time like the present to start!

At eight o'clock (and still without breakfast or even the caffeine jolt of a cup of coffee!) it's time for yoga. With the summer outdoor platform buried under several meters of snow, we are happy to spread our yoga mats in a spacious, heated indoor hall and plunge into our first session of *asanas*, or yogic postures. Starting with the 12-part Sun Salutation that instantly warms us up, we continue with 1.5 hour's worth of postures, including the shoulder stand and head stand for those who can do them, and conclude (at last!) with Savasana or the "corpse pose", which just about captures how we feel after this first strenuous initiation into Sivananda's disciplined brand of yoga.

Ten o'clock. Wide awake but slightly faint with hunger and wondering if we're ever going to eat, at last our first meal of the day—1000 brunch—is served. Ayurvedic, all organic vegetarian, of course. No caffeine. No bacon and eggs. No sugary cinnamon rolls. But delicious just the same with fresh, home-baked bread, steaming spicy vegetable soup and home-made yoghurt with fresh fruit. Now we get to know the other people in our group, most of them regulars from close-by Munich who have their own city Sivananda Centre but frequently skip across the border for a weekend of skiing and yoga. They swear by it! We'll see.

Skiing's on our agenda from eleven til two so we quickly change into our ski clothes, grab our gear and head off together to the nearby Fleckalm, which belongs to the overall Kitzbüheler Ski Circus. Our ski guide is none other than Vasudev, one of the Sivananda staff originally from the province of Salzburg who, we quickly learn, is a fantastic skier from his former life! Tanked full of energy from this morning's yoga session (plus his overall healthy lifestyle), he not only skims swiftly and effortlessly down one slope after another—he throws in a headstand in the snow for good measure!—until soon we're struggling to keep up. No stops for Glühwein and Strüdel, we're here to ski ... and that's what we do without a single pause so that, by the time two o'clock rolls around, we've done six long back-to-back runs and our thighs cry "Enough skiing for today!" Besides, there's another yoga session coming up!

Back to the ashram, quick shower, change clothes and off to afternoon yoga and pranayama. All without lunch! After all, head stands on a full stomach are not advisable. We try out a number of postures named after all manner of living creatures, from crows to cobras and from fish to peacocks. This post-ski session also includes some stretches that work wonders on our cramped muscles. Then there's a short time slot for a sauna or a pre-scheduled massage and—at last!—dinner at six o'clock.

To say we're starving is an understatement! But we feel so stretched and refreshed and the organically grown food tastes so incredibly good that everybody goes back for seconds, sometimes thirds! I also go to seek out the chef and discover that, far from being Indian, he's actually a Kitzbüheler named Martin. When I ask for some recipes, he shares with me the secrets of our easy-to-make supper:

❖ **Spicy Red Dahl with Basmati Rice and Pumpkin-Fennel Vegetables**

❖ **Red Kidney Bean Dahl (4 Portions)**

200 g red kidney beans
1.3 l water
1 laurel leaf
1 Pinch of chili powder
Finely chopped vegetables (e.g. tomatoes, fennel roots, carrots)
2 T Ghee or oil
1 t whole Kreuzkümmel
1 t ground Kreuzkümmel
3 Cardomom capsules
1/2 t Kurkuma
1 T ground ginger
Sea salt
Fresh coriander

Preparation: Wash kidney beans and let them soak in water, preferably overnight. Then cook them, together with the laurel leaf, for about an hour. Meanwhile, cut the vegetables into small cubes, stir them into the dahl and cook for another 30 minutes. Now heat oil in a pan and roast the whole kreuz-kümmel and cardamom briefly, then stir in and roast ground kreuzkümmel, chilli powder and kurkum.

Stir this spice mixture into the dahl, add the freshly ground ginger and sea salt and sprinkle with chopped coriander.

❖ **Fennel-Pumpkin Vegetables (4 Portions):**

2 Fennel roots
1 small Hokkaido pumpkin
4 Tomatoes
3 T Olive oil
1/2 t whole Kreuzkümmel
1/2 t ground coriander
1/2 cinnamon stick
1T ground ginger
1 Pinch of Chili powder
Fresch Parsley
Sea Salt

Preparation: Slice the fennel root and pumpkin into strips and cube the tomatoes. Heat the oil and brown the Kreuzkümmel, ginger and cinnamon stick in a pot. Stir in the coriander and chilli powder. Then add the diced vegetables and simmer for 15 minutes over lowered heat. Season to taste with sea salt and sprinkle with freshly cut parsley.

❖ **Basmatireis (4 Portions):**

200 g Basmatireis
1/2 l Water
2 T Ghee
Sea Salt
1 Laurel leaf

> **Preparation:** Wash the rice. Heat the ghee and roast the rice briefly in it. Then pour the water over it and add seasoning. Cook for 15 minutes and allow to swell for another 15 minutes. Serve hot.
>
> **Guten appetit!**

We have just enough time after dinner to brush our teeth, catch our breath and collect our cushion before the evening programme of meditation and mantra-chanting begins at seven-thirty. During this session, we are reminded that yoga means paying proper attention to the "five points": body posture (asana), breathing (pranayama), relaxation (dharana), nutrition (Ayurvedic vegetarian) and positive thinking/meditation (Vedanta and dhyana). *"Yoga is not itself a religion but an overarching way of life. Thus, it benefits all equally and its effects are far-reaching, indeed life-changing."*

Next day, after skiing, I find myself sitting next to Vasudev in the cable car. On the spur of the moment, I ask him how his years in the ashram have changed his life. He stops what he's doing, looks me straight in the eye with his engaging smile, and says slowly, as if checking out each word with his inner self, *"Yoga really* has *changed my life. It's made me more relaxed ... calmer ... more mindful ... and more balanced."*

After our first full weekend, I can readily imagine that such a simple yet profound way of life *would* make an enormous difference, not only to me but to anyone who has the resolve to practice it fully. And there are a growing number of yoga practitioners throughout the world from Kerala in India to the Sivananda "mother house" near Montreal, Canada. Here in Tyrol alone, a look at the Sivananda Centre's calendar reveals that there are five month-long teacher training courses each year, as well as ayurvedic cooking courses and a host of special events and celebrations. On the spot, I decide to come back for Yoga and Hiking this summer. Then, well, we'll see. Living part-time in an ashram in Tyrol? Why not?

For more details, please contact:

International Sivananda Yoga Retreat Tel. +43 (0)5356 67404
House
Bichlach 40, 6370 Reith/Kitzbühel   Email: www.sivananda.org/tyrol
Tyrol, Austria   www.sivananda.at

Der Adlerweg: On the Eagle's Wings to the Hintersteinersee

Of course, there's more to Tyrol than "just" yoga and skiing and winter. And as the snows melt and the buds bloom, our thoughts turn to one of Tyrol's favorite pastimes—high alpine hiking!

Perhaps one of the best known, and most easily accessible, mountain huts to use as a base point for hiking and climbing tours in the Wilde Kaiser is the Gaudeamushütte (open mid-May through mid-October. Tel. +43 5358 2262).

It's late afternoon when the four of us—Irmgard and Jutta from Munich, Anders from Norway and me—drive up a narrow winding road, passing wooden farmhouses with their window-boxes full of geranium and the sound of cow bells in the pasture, until we arrive at an "end of the road" parking lot. From there it's only about a half hour's walk through the woods and up to the hut. Having been wiped away in one too many avalanches, it now sits out of harm's way on a kind of rock ledge overlooking the valley. We're staying the night in the hut since tomorrow's hike is a fairly long one and we want to get an early start.

We stow our rucksacks and sleeping bags and then grab a good place at an outdoor trestle table, spread out our map and get our bearings. We'll be doing the second day stage of a 126 day long-distance hiking route that spans the whole, highly alpine length of Tyrol. The guide book describes it this way: *"The eagle is the king of the skies. It glides seemingly weightless above it all, gazing down upon pristine Nature from on high. This is the kind of distance and freedom from the trivia of everyday life we will gain through hiking … that's why we've chosen the eagle as the symbol of this trans-Tyrolean high alpine adventure."*

Were we to do it *all*, we would need at least 126 days to go from St Johann in Tyrol, along the flank of the Wilde Kaiser and then through the Brandenberger Alps, the Rofan and Karwendelmountains and finally through the Lech Valley Alps to St. Anton am Arlberg. That's quite a trek that would include climbing a total of 87,000 metres in altitude (eight times the height of Mt Everest, give or take a few thousand metres of elevation), the guide reminds us proudly. It also warns that all who would venture here need not even start without "a sound foundation of fitness and condition, in addition to basic alpine experience, surefootedness and freedom from vertigo." Hmmmm ….

Thank heavens our single day "sampler" will involve a "mere" 6.5 hour hike *Unterwegs im Koasa* (Underway along the Koasa, the cross-country skiing competition route that circles the Wilde Kaiser in winter). All told, we'll be hiking "only" 12 km and climbing up "only" 550 metres (but down almost double) that to arrive at the Hintersteinersee where my daughter is driving up to meet us.

The sun sets and it gets "gemütlich" inside the Gaudeamushütte, what with lots of hikers and climbers, lots of strong Tyrolean dialect and a delicious dinner of Leberknödlsuppe (Liver dumpling soup) followed by the hearty Tiroler G'röstl (potato slivers fried with bacon and onions) and the local Bavarian Weißbier.

Next morning rings in "loud and clear" with our Matrazenlager-sharers up at the crack of dawn and, after a quick coffee, bread and jam breakfast, out into the cool, brisk dawn. We warm up by actually going downhill a little towards the Wochenbrunneralm, but then there's already our first steep stretch up through the mostly evergreen forest towards the Grutenhütte. After an hour or so we reach the Kaiser Hochalm—the Emperor's High Meadows—settled in the 17th century. Stopping for a snack and a break, we absorb the beautiful view and crisp morning sunshine before setting out again slightly downhill through the woods until the marked route splits and we continue on towards the 300-year old Steiner Alm.

Our long traverse brings us past the Gasthof and Chapel of Bärnstatt. Here we're in for a special, if unexpected, treat. It's Sunday and it so happens that this particular Sunday, there's a "meadow mass" being conducted by the local priest. It seems people have come all the way up here especially for this event. And no wonder! The music is provided by a silver-haired trachten-clad couple in their seventies, she playing a harp and he a block flute. Now if that's not Austria …!

We sprawl on the grass and dive into our picknick lunch, then lay back blissfully in the sun, following one of Austria's many touristic invitations to just let go and let your soul swing—"mit der Seele bäumeln"—for a good hour. What's the rush after all?

Finally, though, we do get back on our hiking path towards the Hintersteinersee we know a refreshing swim awaits us. As we hike down through the trees, we can see the sun shimmering invitingly off the surface of the 58 hectare water surface. Impeccably clean, they say it's not even cold (by Tyrolean standards, that is), all of 18° C! After all, it's a glacial lake.

Glacial Lakes: From Schwarzsee to Hintersteinersee

Deep hollows carved out by the receding glaciers millions of years ago, filled with melt water and replenished with rain each season since time immemorial, glacial lakes dot Austria's curvaceous alpine countryside by the hundreds. Some of these lakes, like the Salzkammergut's major ones—are world famous while others, like the Geringer Weyher and the Hintersteinersee, remain a relatively well-kept secret.

Though we have hiked for over six hours to get here, there *is* an easier way. By road, if you know how to find it, Tyrol's *Hintersteinersee* is only about 20 minutes' drive from Kitzbühel. It nestles 900m high on the flank of the *"Kaisergebirge"*—the "Emperor's mountains"—a rock climbers' paradise that towers over the tiny villages of Ellmau and Scheffau.

I got to know these mountains many years ago when married to a Kitzbüheler athlete who was a member of Austria's Olympic team in biathlon (cross-country skiing and marksmanship). Also a bold and avid alpinist, he introduced me to rock climbing right here with the Ellmauer Halt, the range's highest peak (2,234m), the Kopftörlgrat and a few others. But besides these "easy" climbs, he told (literally) hair-raising stories of others, like the time he was doing a traverse of the entire chain of peaks and got caught in a ferocious thunderstorm. Laden as he was with iron carabiners, pitons, etc., the storm made the air all around him sizzle with electricity. Luckily no lightening!

But back to Kitzbühel for a moment. Anyone who skis, golfs or is one of Austria's *haute volé* will know Kitzbühel, and most who know Kitz also know its picturesque *Schwarzsee*—called "Black Lake" because it's a "Moorbad" with healing properties for arthritic joints, etc. A nature preserve, one can walk around it in the summer and cross-country ski across it in the winter. Its ebony surface mirrors the Kaisergebirge and, I reflect that, while 90% of tourists to Tyrol know the Schwarzsee, it's doubtful that even 10% have heard of the Hintersteinersee.

My daughter Chris is half Tyrolean and, since she doesn't have to earn her stripes like I do, she's just driving up here, leisurely as can be! Still, she tells me later, she had to re-trace her route three times to find the single unobtrusive Scheffau turn-off from Route 178, just a secondary road.

She drove up through the community of Scheffau that has existed since 1160 though this area was already settled in the Early Stone Age (3,000 BC) and her tiny winding road could have been laid by the Romans, or even the Celts before them. She relates that, as she wound her way upwards through a cluster of friendly, flower-bedecked Tyrolean chalets, she suddenly realized how steep the grade was! "With that ancient stick-shift VW camper, I downshift from 4th gear to 3rd, then 2nd and finally…umphh!…into 1st just when a group of yodeling mountain bikers whizzed by and razzed me! But we kept on chugging for five more kilometers and finally, made it!" So while she was struggling up, we were struggling down, now to meet in the middle.

Cresting a hill and emerging from the forest, we both arrive at the high wooded hollow of the Hintersteinersee. This lake has a magical quality about it. High-up and secluded, only about five kilometers in circumference and fifty meters deep, it's wooded and steep on the far side and banked by rolling meadows on the near side where a small parking lots marks the end of the road for cars (except the few local residents and overnight guests like me).

The five of us greet each other, set off for the Badestrand (actually a flower-strewn meadow rather that a sand beach), change clothes and tiptoe amidst the rocks into the frigid water. Refreshing as it is, no one can stay in for much more than ten minutes. But that's the ideal cool-down. So we slip back into fresh clothes, lace up our boots and set off for the secluded far end of the lake about 45 minutes away, along with other hikers, local weekend walkers, and families with their dogs and baby strollers. The perfect idyllic afternoon.

Up here it's all Nature preserve: both the lake shore and the lake itself. A German-language sign proclaims: *"This is the private property of TIWAK, the Tyrolean Hydroelectric Company. In order to preserve this jewel of Nature, it is prohibited to boat or fish. Swimming is permitted only in specifically designated areas."* No wonder the lake has drinking water quality!

Arriving at the Pension Maier on a hill overlooking the far tip of the lake, Chris and I are assigned a tiny room with a geranium-bedecked balcony and a panoramic view—all for only €30 (ca. $38), including breakfast! We had considered camping out but can't complain about such a deal and decide to try out our new sleeping bags *inside* tonight. But first for another little pre-supper walk. Chris and I set off for an hour's stroll around this "jewel of Nature," chatting as we go. The other three wave to us from the terrace where they're enjoying coffee and cherry cobbler.

Despite the fact that there's an overflowing dam at one end, the lake's fuller than I've ever seen it, even beyond its banks and covering the trail at one point where we take off our boots and wade through the cool, crystal clear water.

The trail undulates up and down along the steeply wooded side of the lake like a caterpillar on an accordion. Walking, we glance down through the firs and birches to see the lake's rippled surface sparkling like so many multi-faceted diamonds. We're back just in time for a sunset dinner outside.

Sitting on the broad, wind-protected terrace with its plaid tablecloths and orange umbrellas, my gaze wanders over the rose-fenced lawn that serves as a "Liegewiese" (beach) for sunbathers and swimmers—the latter distinctly few in number; after all, this *is* a glacial lake! What's more, most of central Europe is still recovering from some of the worst summer flooding in recent history, which means there have been more showers than sunshine. Still, I console myself that the resulting vivid green, flower-strewn meadows and vibrant foliage is far preferable to the tinderbox forest fires that have devastated the Iberian Peninsula for several weeks now.

Austria is an alpine paradise, I remind myself as I set off along the now quiet promenade. The stroll back is still and leisurely but wet in places as water glides noiselessly from the angled meadows across the path in a thin film, then gurgles into the lake, which is only about 6 cm beneath road level right now. What if there's more rain? I realize that the thought of being stranded up here in paradise rather pleases me! It's s-o-o-o peaceful.

Arriving back at my quaint wooden chalet with its flower boxes filled with pink petunias, I don a Polartec pullover against the evening breeze drifting down from the "Wilder Kaiser," whose serrated peaks are still cloud-shrouded, and find myself a protected corner on the terrace, between pink and white geraniums and a hardy yucca plant.

Frau Maier comes out to greet me and we get to chatting. I learn that this Gasthof and working farm has been in the family for generations and was rebuilt in 1898 after a fire, then renovated and expanded several times so that it now accommodates 22 guests. But her pride and joy is the "Bio-Betrieb"—organic farming done without fertilizers or any genetically manipulated seeds—and the animals that are kept, as in olden times, in the barn underneath the house: 12 milk cows, 8 young steers, 3 calves, 2 sheep, 2 pigs, chickens ... and a house cat.

"Between the animals and the orchards and fields, we get most of our daily food products," she says: "milk, cream, yoghurt, several kinds of cheese, eggs, fresh beef and lamb, fruit, jam ... and, of course, homemade Schnapps, which is one of our specialties. Here we make it from our own apples and pears. Would you like to try some? It's sure to warm you up!" But of course!

Now feeling quite cozily connected with those schnapps-ified apples and pears, I pick up my book by Jack Kornfield, an American-born Buddhist monk, and come across the perfect passage:

"Awakening beyond our self-interest, we find a natural ecology of mind and Nature—fresh, open, joyful, where we are organically connected with all things."

With the lullaby of that thought, I'm off to bed, leaving the balcony door wide open … only to awaken, hours later, to a pre-dawn darkness filled with clouds, softly clinking cow bells and the pitter-patter of rain drops. Cuddling deeper into my sleeping bag, I smile to myself and murmur, "Let it be, let it be."

****

SPRING IN THE COUNTRYSIDE

APRIL: Easter Plus The Beautiful Blue Danube

Happy Easter (Frohe Ostern)

Easter is, chronologically speaking, a moveable feast but one that always falls in March or April. In predominantly Christian Austria Easter many offices and shops close mid-afternoon on Good Friday and do not reopen until the following Tuesday.

Easter Mass at Vienna's Augustinian Church is a very special experience, both because of the heavenly music and because this church is so steeped in history. Located adjacent to the Hofburg, this church dates back to the 14th century and was the parish church of the Hapsburg Imperial Court. Thus, it was the scene of many an imperial wedding: Maria Theresa to Francis Stephen of Lorraine in 1736, Marie Antoinette to Louis XVI of France in 1770, Marie-Louise of Austria to Napoléon in 1810 (by proxy—he didn't show up since she was merely one of the "spoils of war" for him). It was also in this very church that Sisi, the future Empress Elisabeth, married her "prince charming" Emperor Franz Josef on April 24th 1854.

The Choir of the Augustinerkirche is rightly famous and this year's Easter Mass is Große Credo Messe (the Creed Mass). It begins at 1100 but getting a place in the pews means being there by shortly after 1000. As I approach, there is already a hushed sense of reverence. I enter and, as always, am transfixed by the exalted 18ᵗʰ Gothic interior, characteristically "striving towards Heaven" with its slender vertical piers, ribbed vaults and three-story high windows. Although not the effusive Baroque style so typical of many Austrian edifices, its eighteen enormous crystal chandeliers and four storey-high nave windows do make Vienna's other churches look earthbound by comparison.

Sitting in the front pew, I notice that the church is already over half-filled. And no wonder! The choir and 30-piece orchestra is having its last rehearsal so I get an advance ear-full of Mozart's intricate mass. I am taking in the fine gold-lace tiers of the altar, which soars all the way to the ceiling when an elegantly dressed lady comes to greet the elderly couple sitting in the same pew, smilingly saying, "Ein gesegnetes Osterfest"—"a blessed Easter celebration!" I go to light two candles for my daughter and her first child, which will arrive in five months. Now I notice that all the pews are full and people are standing in the side aisles; now the organist is warming up on the enormous rococo organ in the loft—the one on which Bruckner's Mass Nr. 3. in F Minor had its world premier.

I am struck by how different this Easter experience is from the ones I had as a teenager in the American Southwest, when I used to go to the outdoor sunrise services. The people are not "dressed to the nines" in brand new Easter Parade outfits but in modest clothes without hats or gloves ... and they seem to be here out of devotion rather than for a fashion show. Many light candles or sit quietly with the eyes closed as if praying. A priest goes around, manually lighting some 50 candles on the various altars alongside of dozen of potted white chrysanthemums. At 1045 the bells start chiming, the choir falls quiet as the mood intensifies.

Then, at 1100 sharp, all the chandeliers suddenly burst into light at once and festive trumpets signal the start of the Easter High Mass! The next hour-and-a-half is filled with incense and "Hallelujahs" galore to welcome the Resurrection. Mozart's Creed Mass is sung by a 30-strong professional-quality lay choir with four soloists and a 30-piece orchestra. Celebratory! It seems that virtually everyone in the church partakes of the Holy Communion celebrated by four different priests, backed by an Italian Offertorium and Schubert's Post Benedictum! Thus inspired, one comes out into the bright sunshine as if walking on clouds outside St. Peter's Gate!

… but, of course, I've now been inside the church for 2.5 hours on an empty stomach and my earthly body is sending hunger pangs out in all directions to see where the closest food may be. And guess where? From a short 100 hungry meters away beckons Demel's, the k.u.k.—stands for "kaiserlich und königlich" or imperial and royal—pastry makers. My feet lead my body and before long I'm seated on the outdoor terrace area order a capuccino with whipped cream and, of course not the "imitation" Sacher Torte—that would be socially incorrect!—but my chocolate-sweet tooth goes for the "Mohr im Hemd" or "Moor in a Shirt" because that's what the finished product looks like. I add a scoop of ice cream on the side in deference to Demel's modest beginnings.

Mohr im Hemd (Moor in a Shirt)

For six servings:

50g bittersweet cooking chocolate	2 T milk
30g icing sugar	50g crumbled ladyfingers
a. egg yolks	50g hazelnuts or walnuts, roasted & grated
b. egg whites	pinch of salt
3. cl rum	100g melted butter to grease the pan
2 T sugar	3 T sugar for baking forms
50g breadcrumbs	

Chocolate sauce:

150g dark chocolate	½ vanilla pod, cut open
150ml milk	80g soft butter
20g sugar	1 cl cognac
100ml cream	300ml half-whipped cream for decoration

Preparation: Grease several small soufflé molds with melted butter and dust with sugar. Refrigerate (so the mixture can rise without running over the sides). Melt the chocolate in a double boiler. Whisk the egg yolks with rum and icing sugar until fluffy. Pour in the melted chocolate. Whisk the egg whites and sugar and a pinch of salt until half stiff and carefully fold in about 1/3 of the egg whites. Combine the breadcrumbs, ladyfinger crumbs and milk and fold into the mixture, along with the nuts and the rest of the egg whites. Fill the molds ¾ full with the mixture. Fill a deep baking tray with about 2 cm of water(or use a double boiler) and place the molds in water. Bake in a preheated over at 170°C for about 20 minutes.

For the chocolate sauce, heat the milk with the cream, sugar and vanilla pod. Remove the vanilla pod and melt the finely chopped chocolate in the mixture. Whip up the butter and pour in the chocolate mixture, stirring regularly. Pour in some cognac for extra aroma.

Loosen the small cakes from their molds and arrange on plates. Pour on the warm chocolate sauce—that the Moor's "shirt"—and decorate with whipped cream.

Baking time: ca. 20 minutes

Oven temperature: 170°C

Suggested serving options: With a scoop of vanilla or pistachio ice cream, strawberry sauce and hippin (a thin wafer often served with ice cream).

Guten appetit!

Enjoying my calorific dessert along with me, passersby gaze longingly and children point and cry "Ich auch, Eiscreme" (Me too, ice cream!), I browse through the menu and find the short explanatory passage that says, "*In 1786, when everything began, the now-famous Demel was a small ice cream parlour, which soon extended its production to pastries of all kinds … [today, from April to September] we offer our customers Demel ice cream made of natural products in a variety of flavours, always refined with a dash* *of cream: chocolate, vanilla, hazelnut, coffee, pistachio, yoghurt, lemon, strawberry and raspberry. Price €2,00 ($2.50) per scoop."*

The Mystery of "K.u.K"—Solved!

One could see the Hapsburg Empire as one of the world's early attempts at supranationalism, wrapped in endless layers of bureaucracy, ceremony, protocol and military preening. *Fin de siècle* Viennese socialist politician and journalist Viktor Adler described it as "despotism softened by muddle".

In her book, *Europe: An Intimate Journey*, Jan Morris asserted that a Hapsburg trademark was "simplicity allied to total power" but, beyond Franz Josef's own austere lifestyle, the Court and the "Austro-Hungarian Establishment" indulged itself in endless officialdom and adored its medals and sashes, ranks and titles.

Part and parcel of this indulgence was the epithet "K.u.K"— "Kaiserliche und Königliche" or "Imperial and Royal" which referred to the Empire of Austria and the Kingdom of Hungary after the 1867 Compromise that recognized Hungary's Constitution. But this epithet was applied not to people but to business establishments that served the House of Hapsburg. At its height there were many dozens of such enterprises, many of them culinary.

From Vienna to the Romantic Wachau

This picturesque area is part of the legendary Danube Valley that carries this swiftly flowing, second longest river in Europe from its source in Germany's Black Forest through Vienna, then Budapest, Belgrade and at last into the Black Sea, passing altogether through eight countries.

As for cycling, we'll have to wait until the winter tempests abate and the snow melts … ah, but then! Helmut will pick the route, on the condition that it end in a Rip van Winkle vineyard still undiscovered by tourists and with its own rustic wine cellar and picnic table under blooming chestnut trees. I can hardly wait for May!

****

SPRING IN THE COUNTRYSIDE

MAY: Austria's Lipizzaners: A Noble Living Tradition

Horses were to European military history what tanks and transporters are to today's super powers: vehicles to victory and symbols of prestige. A quick survey of Vienna's statues depicting the Austrian Empire at its prime confirms this: Emperors Franz I and Joseph II, Prince Eugen of Savoy, Archduke Karl—all of them on horseback. In terms of pure non-military prestige, Austria's beloved Empress Elisabeth (Sisi) was known to be one of the foremost horsewomen of her day.

So, at the end of the 16th century, it was such "war and peace" reasons that prompted the Hapsburg's decision—as the dynasty was poised at its apogee—to create an Imperial Stud that would lavish unprecedented care and attention on the breeding of a very special kind of horse: the Lipizzaner. This name immortalizes the tiny town overlooking Trieste where stallions were bred and brought up, either for military service or for performance at the world renowned Spanish Riding School, which, though grounded in Spanish equestrian tradition, is actually located in Vienna. Thus, the Lipizzaners were bred to embody the Baroque equestrian ideals of power, agility, intelligence and elegance. Today, though the empire is but a memory, the Lipizzaners tradition lives on, an awe-inspiring legacy.

Still, as world-renowned as the elegant white Lipizzaner stallions of Vienna's Spanish Riding School are, how many people have actually ever *experienced* them live? Either in Austria or elsewhere? Not many. They are a precious rarity.

Since the 1580 founding of the Lipizzaner stud by Inner Austria's Archduke Charles II in Lipizza, a small town high in the hills overlooking Trieste in modern-day Slovenia, the cultivation of this "oldest horse breed in a living tradition," has been carefully nurtured by Europe's aristocracy, especially the Imperial Hapsburg dynasty that ruled for over 600 years. Even today these white stallions represent the epitome of Renaissance equestrianism from Austria's Imperial Baroque Court.

Such perfection takes time, commitment and care. It has to begin somewhere and that is with the breeding and the birth of these future champions … these very special horses renowned for their strong, agile bodies, proud spirits, clever minds and affinity for people.

PIBER AND THE "BIRTHING OF CHAMPIONS"

An early morning in early March. Quiet time in the tiny town of Piber in Austria's "green heart," the province of Styria. The onion dome of the Baroque St Lamprecht's abbey shines with dew. Birds chirp in the still bare populars and box hedges that line the way past the early Baroque Piber castle with its interior court and arcades reminiscent of Italy leading to the entrance of the Federal Stud Farm. Not a soul in sight, not even one of the 239 horses currently resident on the 570 hectares that constitute the Piber Stud.. Terra cotta-coloured roofs, Imperial yellow buildings with white-fenced parameters and the first spring green of the woods and meadows make up the pastel palette of Piber in early spring.

"This is my favorite time of year," says Dr Maximilian ("Max") Dobretsberger, Piber director since 2004, "the time when our Lipizzaner mares—the real treasures of Piber!—give birth. This spring 55 of our 70 mares will bear foals; we already have 16 that we'll see shortly with their mothers.

"And, by the way, these foals can be sponsored. Just this week the granddaughter of Frau Kresch, a local entrepreneurial family from nearby Bärnbach became the proud 'godmother' of a newborn foal who may one day grace the Spanish Riding School." After all, with 68 performing stallions and only another about 25 male colts born each year, the chances are better than winning the lotto! … but it takes time. Lipizzaner stallions mature slowly, reach their peak at between 10 and 20 years of age and can live to be 30 or more."

Before the foals, we tour the stables of the retired stallions, show stallions and, lastly, the breeding stallions who have performed for ten or more years at Vienna's Hofreitschule and on tours around the world. Fabulous to see and stroke up close, their names, indicating which of the six stallion families they belong to, ring with romance: Siglavy Mantua (1979), Neapolitana-Primavera (1979), Pluto Presciano (1984), Maestoso Basonizza (1985), and Conversano Toscana I (1984). Enthralled by Conversano, Max calls him "a dream horse, noble, perfectly proportioned, just look at those expressive, liquid brown eyes … and he's so friendly!" Turns out he's the half-brother of Conversano Calcedona, the current SRS "Capriole" specialist (see below).

The six breeding stallions are reaping the rich rewards for all their years of hard work. Now, in this idyllic equestrian "Freudenhaus", they have nothing to do but mate with the most sumptuous mares and enjoy the fruits of their former labours. Still, their testosterone makes them 'testy.' "While the mares spend their time peacefully together in the same paddock, stallions have to be kept in separate stalls," Max says. "Whenever there are ladies around, the guys will fight." That's ostensibly why the Spanish Riding School is "for gentlemen only" even though the ladies—both horses and riders—might be equally talented. It's "the weight of tradition," as patriarchal as that may sound in these days of female equal rights.

After passing by another paddock to meet the "Mädels"—nine young five-year-old mares who will be next in line to breed—we make our way up the gentle hill towards the mature mare's enclosure where, indeed, they are peacefully grazing and enjoying the early spring sunshine while staff clean and rake the gravel path. Most of the mares are quite visibly pregnant and thus taking it easy prior to giving birth. But the amazing thing is how quickly they do it! Although not allowed to view an actual foaling, despite my wheedling, Max, himself a doctor of veterinary medicine, tells me that, "because horses are flight animals, protracted labour is virtually unheard of. Births usually take no more than 20 minutes … and often occur in the stillness of the night. So our staff is on duty around the clock."

But Calcedona, a first-time mother, has chosen today's lunch break instead so by the time we arrive, her dark brown filly is all of 45 minutes old! Amazingly, she's already tottering around on stilt-like legs, switching her short tail and nuzzling her somewhat spent mother for milk, the first colostrum that contains vital antibodies against a host of diseases and thus serves as a liquid, oral vaccine. "It's her first birth so she's still having contractions; future pregnancies will be easier," Max assures me as we make a photo of him with another mother and foal who are sunning in a large paddock.

Stallions begin their procreative roles at about ten years old while mares start at five and usually bare between twelve and sixteen foals during their reproductive lifetimes. Sixteen, it so happens, is also the number of children borne by 18th century Austrian Empress Maria Theresia who holds an Imperial maternal record of sorts—but for mares—with each pregnancy taking about 333 days out of 365 in each year, this means they are pregnant for over half of their 25-year average life span!

To my question of whether the mares have been relegated to a role as glorified breeding machines, I am told that this is the way it happens in nature. But this remains an open issue in my mind. I cannot but compare the lives of the stallions who "perform" before thousands of dazzled spectators ... while the equally superb mares are bred to "perform" continually yet quietly out of sight in Piber where they are "decked" one short month after giving birth and definitively separated from their foals after only six months, by which time they are already, once again, five months pregnant. And, although I am assured that mothers and foals no longer recognize each other after separation, I cannot help but draw comparisons between these highly sensitive and intelligent mothers, horses on the one hand, humans on the other. Recalling the anguish of the 17-year old Austrian Empress Elisabeth when her first child Sophie was forcibly removed from her, I wonder if this 'tradition' is the equestrian equivalent to the old German "Kinder, Küche, Kirche" ... or simply another example of highly rational, economically sound long-term strategic planning with the mares as means to an end.

Adopt a Lipizzaner! In an initiative to bring this living tradition closer to the people, make the Piber stud farm more accessible to the public and obtain additional resources for expert care of the horses, individual and corporate contributors can now sponsor new-born foals and full-grown SRS stallions for the following amounts:

- **Sponsor a foal:** € 450/year (individuals) or € 1,000/year (businesses) at the Piber Stud farm.

- **Sponsor a SRS Stallion:** € 10,000/year for one of the 68 stallions at the Riding School in Vienna.

- **Sponsors' Benefits:** Although the "adopted" horses remain at Piber or the Spanish Riding School, where they are trained and/or perform, sponsors benefit from special visiting rights, free tickets for performances and "behind the scenes" visits to observe the trainers working with the horses—a first in the school's history. Individual sponsors also receive a personalized certificate with their horse's photo while corporate sponsors will be listed with the firm's logo on a plaque erected outside the stalls and acknowledged on the stud farm's homepage.

- **Role Model Sponsors** include former US Ambassador to Austria, William Lee Lyons Brown, the first honourary sponsor in return for his patronage over the last few years, as well as Britain's Queen Elizabeth II who has expressed "private" interest.

You never know! Your foal might grow up to be one of the next generation's Spanish Riding School star performers. Conversano Calcedona did!

FROM FRISKY FOAL TO SRS STAR:
CONVERSANO CALCEDONA

Back in 1986, a *star* foal was born—the Lipizzaner *Conversano Calcedona*. "You can never be absolutely sure which mating may prove to be a 'marriage made in heaven' that produces a magnificent offspring like 'Calce'," says Chief Rider Riegler, "but our Piber Stud takes care to ensure that the best lineage is there." The rest is up to the horses, and their sharp-eyed grooms and trainers who scrutinize them as the new foals mature, to see which ones have star quality."

'Calce' had the right stuff right from the beginning. He was both clever and capricious; and he had the temperament to make his presence known and respected within the herd. A very frisky foal, he took naturally to the rocky high pastures and was both swift and agile in his movements. While he made his way up the hierarchy of same-year foals, he was not aggressively combative and, a key attribute, he appreciated people and seemed eager to learn from them.

So when the selection was made of stallions to be initiated into the SRS training, he was one of them, along with four others. In the following years, 'Calce' proved to be a superb, if sometimes mischievous, student, one who preferred the "School above the Ground" with its demanding jumps.

Today, 'Calce' is one of the top SRS performers whose specialty is the 'Capriole,' in which the stallion leaps, bringing all four legs simultaneously into the air, then lashes out with its hind legs—originally a protective measure during combat but today a feat that brings forth applause.

Behind the scenes, relaxing in his spacious stall after a Sunday morning performance in Vienna, 'Calce' exhibits some of the traits that have made him who he is. Though he doesn't know me—I am introduced by his rider who opens the stall door, calls him and gives him a little sugar (which he sucks on instead of swallowing whole as most horses might do)—he immediately comes right up to me, full of friendly curiosity, and nuzzles my shoulder.

His rider, Hans Riegler, and I talk for quite some time about both horses and riders and how vital it is to be temperamentally harmonious and evolve as one. And, even as an outsider, I cannot help but sense the intimate bond that exists between the two of them. When we finally leave, I feel I've found two new friends: both *Conversano Calcedona* and Hans.

Spanish Tradition. Today's elegant Austrian Lipizzaners come from a long Spanish tradition. Their precursors, called "Spanish Karster," were bred using Spanish horses, as well as Italian ones with Spanish ancestry, and others from as far afield as Germany, Denmark and Arabia. They were bred both for survival in close-quarters combat and for prestige value in Europe's Baroque courts. Amazingly, the Lipizzaner were good at both.

In breeding, their appearance, as well as temperament, performance and stamina, were critically important. Recalling that the 16th century Hapsburg Empire spanned Europe, from **Hungary** in the East to **Portugal** in the West, multiple cultures contributed to today's Lipizzaner tradition.

Austrian Travails: For over 330 years (1580-1915), the "Court Stud Karster" in modern day Slovenia was the Austrian imperial family's private stud. But persistent conflicts and the gradual decline of Hapsburg power put an end to this three-centuries old stud after Austria's defeat in World War I. Even though Lipizzaners were originally bred for use in combat, the vicissitudes of wars that Austria lost—from the 19th century Napoleonic Wars to both 20th century World Wars—wrought havoc on the horses, too. Many mares miscarried; many others died while being moved from Lippiza on the Austro-Italian front to Laxenburg just outside Vienna after 1915. Not only that. The Italians, who fought on the Allied side, demanded return of over half the herd. It took until 1920 to move the remaining Lipizzaners—less than 100 at their low point—to Piber in modern day Styria.

The Second World War fall of Austria in April 1945 resulted in the Lipizzaners' legendary odyssey to Czechoslovakia where they were saved by the intervention of US General Patton only at the last moment from becoming horsemeat for starving war survivors. Finally, the Lipizzaners were brought home to Piber and, since then, peace in Europe plus Austria's neutrality has enabled this noble tradition to be nurtured and the herd expanded to over 250 in 2007.

Piber Stud: "Lipizzaner Family Life" in Styria. Today's life is idyllic in comparison to the hardships brought on by the various wars that ravaged Europe. While the pleasure of mating is one of the rewards awaiting the "best and the brightest" of the Spanish Riding School's stallions, these pairings are, without a doubt, "arranged marriages." Each mating is carefully planned, carried out and monitored during the first month after foaling. Modern technological equipment makes it possible to know within a few weeks when the mare is pregnant. Gestation takes just under a year (333 days)—which means that mares are pregnant for 11 out of 12 months of every calendar year for 12-16 consecutive years! Foaling occurs between January and June. The dark-coated male foals ("geldings") receive double-barreled names like "Neapolitano-Aquilea" to reflect the lineage of the father's and mother's side. The fillies, surprising to learn, remain nameless until the following year.

The first six months is devoted to cultivating the foal's trust, especially with its human counterparts (e.g. stable boys, trainers). Only after half a year are the foals separated from their mothers—this is done all at once with no slow weaning and put into yearling herds. The young horses start expressing their own personality, especially once the herds are gender-separated into geldings and fillies at 12 months.

A three-year period of idyllic freedom in Styria's alpine pastures allows the young horses to cultivate their strength and agility, as well as a sense of hierarchy within the herd. At four years old, these leaders are most likely to be chosen to perform with the Spanish Riding School in October of each year when selections are made.

Being selected is an "honour" that drastically alters their heretofore idyllic lives when they are moved to the discipline of the Riding School in Vienna. There they will spend up to 20 years learning to master the intricacies of the equestrian schools on and above the ground. The finished product is a spectacle to behold!

HORSE SHOES AND RIDING BOOTS
A Live Gala Performance at Vienna's Hofreitschule

Crisp, winter morning with a dusting of new snow in Austria's capital. The anticipation is tangible as a small crowd gathers inside the welcome warmth of the Hofburg's elegant Spanish Riding School—allegedly "the oldest and most beautiful equestrian hall in the world, built by architect Fischer von Erlach in 1735, which remains dedicated to Renaissance horsemanship" This is, after all, a gala performance and only one of a dozen or so performances that the Lipizzaners will offer this winter in Vienna. There will be seven "figures", most with riders, some without. And a total of 68 horses.

Amidst excited whispers, we mount the stairs and take our place between the two-storey-high Ionic columns that encircle the grandiose Spanish Riding School. Three exquisite chandeliers hang suspended, brightly illuminating the "stage" which consists of Zen-sparse, finely combed sand that is flush with the first-class Loges at the far end of the 80-meter long hall. A mammoth portrait of founder Emperor Charles VI adorns the far end of the hall behind the loges. Almost like the Opera!

The music starts. No Kentucky blue grass or Montana rodeo music here. Instead selections from the European classical tradition: Boccherini, Strauss, Zirhrer, Bizet, Chopin, Laner, Riedinger, and, of course, Mozart in this 400th anniversary year.

High time now. The horses arrive. "Youth before beauty," the moderator intones in multiple languages. That means we will see the young stallions first. An "all guy thing": the horses are all stallions and the riders all male. Perhaps this, too, will change but for now, they are not to be "distracted". Eight incredibly light, elegant young stallions enter the oblong ring from just beneath where we sit—two of them dark, three gray-mottled, three silver-grey sliding towards white. Riedinger's "Festive Entrance" accompanies them. Is any one having a debut today? We don't know.

But the riders look like land-locked admirals in their seafaring cocked hats, brown tailcoats, white buckskin breeches, knee-high riding boots and kid gloves. Sitting ramrod-straight and solemn, as the horses stride single file center, the riders raise their hats in a slow-motion gesture of acknowledgement, the audience applauds, and—oops! the two dark colts shy abruptly at the noise! That's the 'flight instinct' that will be curbed over the coming years ... but it makes the audience empathetic with their learning curve.

"Well, ladies and gentlemen" says the moderator, "this is the Dancing School for Horses. You have to start at the beginning ... and some dancers are shy." The audience nods, perhaps remembering. "Still, this is the 'Star Ensemble'", he says. "Only the best." Imperial tradition.

For the next two hours, a total of 68 increasingly mature stallions perform an ever more demanding programme where the horse's physical conditioning, strong will and readiness to learn are decisive: all the gaits and figures of the "high equestrian school", including walk, trot, gallop, pas de deux, passage, half-pass and finally the quadrille.

The programme next elevates itself to the "school above the ground" where only the most extraordinary of stallions remain. Strength, suppleness, power and elegance are the keynotes here. Performing to the lilting tones of Strauss' "Vienna Blood", the horses, in most cases including their riders, perform the most demanding classical Baroque figures. From dainty pirouettes, they progress to the Levade, the Courbette and, finally, the Capriole, in which the stallion leaps, bringing all four legs simultaneously into the air, then lashing out with its hind legs—originally a protective measure during combat.

The performance concludes with a 20-minute long, intricately patterned "School Quadrille." We are transported back in time to the splendor of a slow-motion quadrille in the high Baroque Court of Empress Maria Theresia. Only this time it's eight sleek stallions who dance, nodding their noble heads to the polonaises and gavottes, flicking their manes and flowing white tails for the gallop passacaglias, following close-knit and single file in rhythmed unison or criss-crossing one another in a syncopated trot that recalls a dainty butterfly in flight. By the time it ends with the riders tapping their hats at the end of the traditional closing "Radetzky March," we are mesmerized.

Carriages and "Kaiserschimmel"

Of course, not every Lipizzaner ends up at the Spanish Riding School. What of the others? During the Hapsburg's heyday, a tradition of elegant imperial carriages drawn by a pair of "Kaiserschimmel"—imperial white horses—was born to show off the city's aristocracy on its outings through the Prater, etc. The carriage museum in Piber features an amazing variety: from Imperial K&K to Prince Rudolf's spartan hunting carriage to an oft-used "marriage carriage" with large, gold-gilt wheels.

Back in Vienna, more modest versions of such Lipizzaner-drawn carriages are commonplace even today! They stand at the ready outside Vienna's St Stephen's Cathedral and in front of the Hofburg Palace to clip-clop visitors through the inner city's winding lanes, complete with commentary by their tradition-clad, dialect-laden coachmen. In fact, there is a special dish dedicated to these hardy souls who work through the winter.

Fiaker Goulash

The year 1693 marked the licensing of what remains to this day a colourful Viennese tradition: the official hackney—or 'Fiaker'—coachman. These authentic drivers still don their traditional costumes consisting of houndstooth trousers, velvet jacket and top hat to ply the historic inner city's narrow cobblestone lanes with their pairs of romantic, horse-drawn carriages. Just as unique—and spicy—is the Hungarian-based 'Gulyas' that warmed them on cold winter nights. By the way, this is one of the dishes that gets better with time so, by all means, serve it as a 'leftover'!

Ingredients:

2 lbs of beef for roasting	*1 ½ lbs onions*	*2 T oil or shortening*
2 T sweet paprika powder	*1 T vinegar*	*3 cups (24 oz) beef stock*
2 crushed garlic cloves	*pinch of marjoram*	*½ tsp ground caraway*
1 T tomato paste	*4 eggs*	*4 frankfurters*
Salt, pepper	*4 pickles (garnish)*	

Rinse the beef under cold water, pat dry with a paper towel and cut into large cubes. Peel the onions and chop them finely. Pour oil into a large skillet and sauté onions until golden brown. Sprinkle with sweet paprika powder. Add vinegar and several tablespoons of beef stock.

*Now add the cubed meat and spices. Reduce the heat, cover and simmer for about 1 ½ hours, stirring frequently and adding beef stock as required. When the meat is tender, add the remaining beef stock, tomato paste and crushed garlic. Simmer for 10 more minutes and season to taste. Spoon goulash into soup bowls and garnish with a fried egg, frankfurter and a gherkin cut in fan form. **Bon apétit!***

Demel's Delights: Sweet-tooth tourists may prefer something more decadent. If so, just a short fiaker ride from the Hofburg's Spanish Riding School, is the K und K—for Königliche und Kaiserliche (i.e. royal and imperial)—Patisserie called Demel's where sweets addictions are indulged.

Squeezing in amongst the old-fashioned marble-topped tables filled with elegant Austrians sipping their myriad of different varieties of coffee and downing delectable pastries, we choose a classical Austrian specialty with an Austrian dialect name: "Powidltascherl" or "plum pockets". In an attempt to merge sweetness with health, Austrian desserts do make ample use of fruit: apricots for the famous Sacher Torte and plums for Kaiserschmarrn and these delightful "pockets".

Plum Pockets—Powidltascherl

Potato Dough Ingredients:

1 lb cooked salad potatoes	*4-5 oz flour*	*pinch of salt*
2 T semolina	*1 ½ oz butter*	*2 egg yolks*
1 tsp grated lemon rind		

Filling Ingrediens:

5 oz plum jam	*1-2 tsp sugar*	*pinch of cinnamon*
2 T rum	*1 egg white*	*2 oz melted butter*
3 T bread crumbs	*2 T powdered sugar, sifted (as decoration)*	

Boil, peel and dice mature baking potatoes. Let cool. Combine salt, flour, semolina, butter, egg yolks and grated lemon rind in a large bowl to form a smooth dough. Let stand for ca. 30 min.

Mix plum jam with cinnamon and sugar. Roll dough out on a floured surface to about ¼-inch thickness. Cut out circles and 3 inches in diameter. Place a teaspoon of prune filling in the center of each circle and brush edges with egg white. Fold over and press edges firmly together. Simmer in salted water for 7-9 min.

Brown bread crumbs in butter, Transfer pockets from water to skillet with a slotted spoon. Shake pan to cover pockets. Sprinkle with powdered sugar before serving. Bon apétit!

We decide that the best way to crown these two Lipizzaner experiences—first in Piber, then in Vienna—will be to undertake an overnight trailride ourselves, using Piber as a base. Though we aren't the caliber of riders to even think of Lipizzaners, we do ask the owner of the Piber Stud Farm-linked Gasthof Bardel and learn that this is feasible. "But you should be at least be a practiced rider first," he says, "otherwise, all you'll have is aches and pains rather than a memorable adventure." We agree and set a date for May, giving our bodies two months to get in shape!

****